HOW TO GROW IN YOUR CHRISTIAN LIFE

FIRST STEPS for the NEW CHRISTIAN

HOW TO GROW IN YOUR CHRISTIAN LIFE

CUMBERLAND HOUSE
NASHVILLE, TENNESSEE

Contents

Preface

To begin to live the Christian life in all its fullness, we must first grasp all that is promised to us and required of us by God's Word, and then begin to apply it.

First Steps for the New Christian —*How To Grow In Your Christian Life* was initially developed and taught at Moody Bible Institute in Chicago. For over forty years it has been part of a Bible correspondence course for the External Studies Division of Moody Bible Institute. In fact, year after year, it is Moody's most popular book with tens of thousands sold!

Now this incisive and insightful book is available for personal or group inductive Bible study to help new believers apply the principles of God's Word and come to enjoy the Christian life as God intended it.

How To Grow In Your Christian Life truly does offer virtually everything you need to grow and deepen your Christian life!

— *The Publisher*

Introduction

Being a Christian may not be easy, especially if you are a new believer. But it can and should be a thrilling and rewarding experience!

How To Grow In Your Christian Life is a concise, simple, yet sound study on assurance of salvation, forgiveness from sin, and how to form good habits for spiritual growth.

Also covered are the significance of baptism and communion, how to get the most out of Bible reading and prayer, dealing with temptation, being a witness, and how to choose a church.

This book and others in the *First Steps for the New Christian* series provides study materials on the various aspects of living a full, rich Christian life. Other titles in the series currently include:

How to Begin Your Christian Life
How to Understand Your Bible
How to Know God's Will

Additional titles in the *First Steps for the New Christian* series are forthcoming.

Because these materials were initially used both as classroom and correspondence school texts, the style is that of a teacher — guiding, challenging, directing, stimulating, and raising questions as well as providing answers.

The content of this edition is taken from an adult credit cours from Moody Bible Institute External Studies Division. For information on how you might take this and other courses for credit, write for a free catalog to:

Moody External Studies
Moody Bible Institute
820 North La Salle
Chicago, IL 60610

1

*A*ssurance of Salvation

"These things have I written . . . that you may know that you have eternal life" (1 John 5:13).

CAN YOU BE SURE YOU ARE SAVED?

A Bible teacher said to his class, most of whom were professing Christians: "Please answer these two questions: Are you a Christian? If so, how do you know you are saved?" Here are some of the answers he received:

"I hope so."

"I do the best I can to be a Christian."

"I won't know till I get to heaven—if I do get there. I wouldn't presume to say I know for sure."

"I think I'm just as good as most church members I know."

"I'm trying to believe in Christ, but am not sure I know how."

"I'm afraid there's no hope for me; I'm too great a sinner."

"I hope I'm not a heathen!"

"I wish I knew for sure!"

Must we only hope and strive and wish, or perhaps despair, about being saved? What is the answer?

Every person can know that he or she has eternal life because of (1) the direct statements from the Word of God, (2) the witness of the Holy Spirit in the heart, and (3) the outward evidence of a new life which indicates a change within.

DIRECT STATEMENTS FROM THE WORD OF GOD

Here are a few of the many verses that tell what the Bible says about assurance of salvation: "Verily, verily, I say unto you, he that hears my word, and believes on him that sent me, has everlasting life, and shall not come into condemnation [or, judgment]; but is passed from death unto life" (John 5:24). "These things have I written unto you, that you may know that you have eternal life, even unto you that believe on the name of the Son of God" (1 John 5:13 ASV). "In hope [or, in accordance with the promise] of eternal life, which God, that cannot lie, promised before the world began" (Titus 1:2).

John 5:24 shows us that, if we believe in Christ as our Savior, we have eternal life. First John 5:13 shows us that the Bible has been written to give us assurance of that life. And Titus 1:2 shows us that this life has been given to us by God, who cannot lie.

Having seen this, you still may ask:

CAN WE BELIEVE THE BIBLE?

Since our assurance rests on what the Bible says, we must believe that the Bible is the very Word of God if we are to have assurance of salvation. How, then, may we be sure that the Bible is his Word? The following facts give us the answer by showing evidence within the Bible and from experience.

1. The Bible claims to be the Word of God

Throughout Scripture, the Bible claims to be the Word of God. Expressions such as "God said," "God spoke," and "the Lord commanded" are found throughout the Old Testament. (See Genesis 1:3; Exodus 20:1; Joshua 14:5; or glance at the first verse in several chapters in Leviticus.) In the New Testament the Lord Jesus and his apostles testified to the fact that the Bible is God's Word. (See, for example, Luke 24:27, 44; John 10:35; Acts 1:16, 17:2; 2 Timothy 3:16; 2 Peter 1:21.)

2. The Bible is proved to be the Word of God

a. *Unity.* The words of God recorded in the Bible were spoken over a period of about 1600 years (see Hebrews 1:1–2). God spoke through men of different countries and languages, of different occupations and walks of life. Yet the Bible is *one* book. It presents the one theme of redemption throughout its pages. It shows that God spoke

11

through "holy men of God" as they were "moved by the Holy Spirit" (2 Peter 1:21).

b. *Fulfilled prophecy.* Hundreds of Old Testament prophecies about the coming Savior, the Jew, and the Gentile nations have been literally fulfilled. Only God could have known these things before they came to pass. For example, about 700 B.C. Isaiah foretold the virgin birth of Christ, and Micah prophesied that the Messiah would be born in Bethlehem (see Isaiah 7:14; Micah 5:2).

c. *Archaeology.* Archaeology confirms the Bible and silences the critics. The ruins of the walls of Jericho have been found, verifying the Bible record of the destruction of that ancient city (see Joshua 6); and this is just one of many such proofs that the biblical record is true.

d. *The test of time.* The Bible has stood the test of the ages. Sword and flame, atheism and paganism, cold indifference and false prophets—all have failed to destroy the Word of God.

e. *Universal demand.* The Bible is the bestselling book. Millions upon millions have read it through the years, and millions read it still.

f. *Denunciation of sin.* Evil in all of its forms is neither hidden nor tolerated in the Holy Scriptures. Whereas humans often overlook sin, making heroes out of tyrants or pretenders, the Bible always treats it openly and honestly. An illustration of this is seen in the sin of Moses that kept him from leading Israel into Canaan. He was perhaps the greatest of Old Testament characters; yet God faithfully portrayed his failure (see Numbers 20:7–13), as well as his life of obedience (Exodus 17:5–7).

g. *The power to change lives.* God's Word has the power to transform lives utterly marred by sin. George Müller is a famous example. Saved from a life of iniquity, he founded and operated Christian orphanages in England, altogether by faith.

We have seen that the Bible is the Word of the living God, and it is this Word that tells us we "may know that we have eternal life." We can know that we are saved by believing the Bible, which says: "He that hears my word, and believes on him that sent me, has everlasting life" (John 5:24).

Our second reason for assurance of salvation is:

THE WITNESS OF THE HOLY SPIRIT

"The Spirit himself bears witness with our spirit, that we are the children of God" (Romans 8:16 ASV).

1. What does this mean?

Who is the Holy Spirit, and how does he bear "witness with our spirit"? In the first place, the Holy Spirit is a person, a member of the Holy Trinity—Father, Son, and Holy Spirit. He is not a mere influence as some incorrectly believe. The Bible identifies him as *God*; and he is co-existent, co-equal, and co-eternal with the Father and with the Son.

The Christian's body is "the temple of the Holy Spirit" (1 Corinthians 6:19–20). And in every experience as redeemed children of God, believers should be conscious of his presence and power—whether in work or play, in Bible study, prayer, worship, or service. "This is how we know that we dwell in him [i.e., God], and he in us: because he has given us of his Spirit" (1 John 4:13).

Thus it is that the Holy Spirit himself bears "witness with our spirit, that we are children of God." But let us examine the Scriptures further to see how this truth is made real in our experience.

2. How the Holy Spirit witnesses in the believer

a. *The Holy Spirit is the believer's teacher.* Before he went to the cross, the Lord Jesus told his disciples: "The Holy Spirit, whom the Father will send in my name, he shall teach you all things, and bring to your remembrance all that I said unto you" (John 14:26 ASV; see also John 15:26–27; 16:12–15).

b. *The Holy Spirit is the believer's comforter.* The Greek word translated "Comforter" in John 14:16 is *parakletos* which means that the Holy Spirit is "called to one's side" to aid. The word was used in a court to denote a counsel for the defense, an advocate. In its widest sense the word means "comforter." When Jesus promised that the Holy Spirit would be *another* comforter, the Greek word for "another" implies another of the same sort as himself, not another of a different kind (See also John 14:26, 15:26, 16:7).

c. *The Spirit of God is the believer's guide.* In John 16:13 we read "But when he, the Spirit of truth is come, he will guide you into all truth." The Greek word for "guide" in this passage means "to lead the way" and is used of guiding the blind in Matthew 15:14. The Spirit of God takes believers by the hand, as it were, and leads them step by step into the truths of Scripture. (See also Romans 8:1, 14.)

d. *The Spirit is the believer's helper and intercessor.* We do not know what to pray for as we ought, so the Spirit of God aids us in our prayer life. In fact, he makes intercession for us. Note what Paul says of the Spirit's ability in this regard. He knows his own mind, he knows our hearts and he knows the will of God. His work as intercessor is therefore perfect.

Have you experienced the joy of the presence of the Holy Spirit? Have you sensed his help in making the Bible live for you in a new way? Have you sensed a new awareness of his influence in your life? If so, then here is another evidence of the assurance of your eternal salvation (Romans 8:16).

The third reason for our assurance of salvation is:

A NEW LIFE—A TRANSFORMED LIFE

A transformed life is the result of our belief in and obedience to God's Word and of the working of the Holy Spirit. "If any man be in Christ, he is a new creature: old things are passed away; behold, all things are become new" (2 Corinthians 5:17).

If we have been redeemed by God's grace, we know that we are new creatures in Christ because we have a new attitude toward sin; we are prompted by new desires; we seek new friends; and our very lives bear "the fruit of the Spirit." This is the transformed life.

1. A new attitude toward sin

Christians no longer serve their own desires as they once did. Old things become new, and Christ is magnified in their hearts and lives. The Lord Jesus becomes the new center of attraction. Sin becomes abhorrent, and they hate themselves when they commit it (Romans 7:19–20). This is the work of the Holy Spirit in the lives of Christians; for he convicts of sin, and leads the wayward child of God to confess that sin. Thus joy and peace are restored.

2. New desires and new friends

Those who trust Christ are new creatures. The Lord Jesus brings new desires and a new way of life. New believers will sense a growing desire to seek the companionship of Christians instead of unbelievers. Old habits and evil desires will lose their power and influence. This is another confirmation of the assurance of salvation that "all things are become new" (2 Corinthians 5:17).

3. "The Fruit of the Spirit"

"By their fruits you will know them" (Matthew 7:20).

These words were spoken by Christ himself. And the apostle Paul explained that "the fruit of the Spirit" will be manifest in the daily lives of obedient children of God. Their family, friends, business associates—all will see that they have "been with Jesus" (Acts 4:13). It is a searching test; but it proves the reality of faith. "The fruit of the Spirit is love, joy, peace, longsuffering, kindness, goodness, faithfulness, meekness, self-control; against such there is no law" (Galatians 5:22–23 ASV).

4. Assurance confirmed by Christian growth

Perhaps you are thinking: "I'm only a newborn in Christ. I haven't experienced this high standard in my daily living. May I still have assurance of salvation?"

Yes, eternal salvation rests in our Lord's finished redemption, not in anything we can do (Titus 3:5). We do not have to experience this high standard in order to have assurance of salvation. We do have to "press on toward the goal unto the prize of the high calling of God in Christ Jesus" if we want his best now and his reward when we stand before the judgment seat of Christ. (See Philippians 3:14 ASV; 1 Corinthians 3:11–15.)

SURETY OF SALVATION

Salvation in Christ is sure! The Bible says so; the Holy Spirit tells us we are Christ's; and our transformed lives, changed by the power of God, tell us so. Let us believe it and rejoice in it. "These things have I written unto you, that you may know that you have eternal life, even unto you that believe on the name of the Son of God" (1 John 5:13 ASV).

2

Forgiveness of Sin

"You will cast all their sins into the depths of the sea" (Micah 7:19).

You may now be thinking: "I'm happy that I have assurance of salvation, and I know my redemption is as certain as my unchanging God. But I'm afraid I'll sin. Won't this affect my assurance of salvation?"

To find the answer to this question and similar problems, consider two aspects of the forgiveness of sin: (1) eternal forgiveness—God's forgiveness of the sinner the moment he or she believes the gospel; and (2) "parental forgiveness"—our heavenly Father's forgiveness of the child who is in the family, "the household of God" (Ephesians 2:19).

ETERNAL FORGIVENESS FOR THE PENALTY OF SIN

1. The problem: a holy God and sinful people

God is holy, even as the prophet wrote, saying to him, "You are of purer eyes than to behold evil, and cannot look on iniquity" (Habakkuk 1:13). Sin is abhorrent to God. It cannot abide in his presence. However, he loves the sinner, and he created us for fellowship with himself.

God's righteous nature demands that sin be punished. He cannot excuse sin as you and I might. That is why Adam and Eve were cast out of the Garden of Eden. The punishment God meted out for sin was death, both physical and spiritual. (See Genesis 3:16–24; Romans 6:23.)

Sin entered the world through Adam, who, with full knowledge of the penalty, deliberately disobeyed God (1 Timothy 2:14). Thus mankind became a sinner by choice and by practice. Every person since then, having descended from Adam, has inherited the same corrupt nature; and when left to their own devices, follow in the same wicked way (Romans 3:9–12).

What a contrast! On the one side there is the absolutely holy God, and on the other utterly sinful man. The great chasm between is death. This gulf seems uncrossable. In view of the eternal, unchanging holiness of God and the inability of man to gain merit with his Creator, the children of Adam are completely bankrupt before the Lord.

It was Job who, in acknowledging his helplessness before Jehovah, asked, "How can man be just with God?" (Job 9:2 ASV).

2. The answer: "Christ died for the ungodly" (Romans 5:6)

God in his love provided an answer in his Son, Jesus Christ (John 3:16). To justify man before God, a perfect, sinless sacrifice was needed to make payment for sin. Yet such a person had to be infinite in order to provide the infinite sacrifice needed to redeem all repentant sinners and deliver them from the guilt of all sin—past, present, and future. All this and much more we have in Christ, for he is God and he is our perfect substitute. (See 2 Corinthians 5:21.)

As it was with Adam of old, the guilt of sin lay heavily upon us; and the penalty was death. But God in his love provided Christ to take our place on the cross. He died that we might live. Before God the penalty of our sin was fully paid. We are justified. We are declared righteous (Romans 5:6–11.)

3. The blessing of eternal forgiveness

A mind at perfect peace with God
Oh, what a word is this!
A sinner reconciled to God
This, this indeed, is peace!
By nature and by practice far
How very far from God!
Yet now by grace brought nigh to him
Through faith in Jesus' blood.
So nigh, so very nigh to God
I cannot nearer be;
For, in the person of his Son,
I am as near as he.
So dear, so very dear to God

More dear I cannot be;
The love wherewith he loves the Son
Such is his love to me.
—Catesby Paget

This is God's message to you. He wants you to know the peace and joy that his salvation provides, because the burden of your sin has been rolled away.

Moreover, in his sight, your sins are blotted out and your position is that of a child without spot or blemish. "By one offering he has perfected them forever that are sanctified" (that is, set apart for him) (Hebrews 10:14).

> In the sight of God, through the value of the blood of Christ, I am perfected forever—not a spot on me. . . . I need to be cleansed in the blood of Christ only once [for the penalty of sin]. It is not only one Sacrifice on the cross, but it is also one purging, that is, one application. . . . [See Hebrews 9:14; 10:14–18.] The moment the precious blood of Christ was applied to you by the Holy Spirit . . . you were . . . "perfected forever"—not a spot on you, and there never will be.[1]

This is true because the Lord Jesus Christ fully paid the penalty for your sins. The trial for your guilt was held at the cross, and by faith in Christ you are freed from the penalty of your sins. God as judge has forgiven you once for all in Christ. He is no longer your judge; he is your Father. You are no longer treated as a

---

1   Alfred Mace, *Addresses* (New York: Loizeaux Bros., 1942), p. 34.

sinner on trial, but as a child under the parental care of a loving Father.

This does not mean that you are free from sin or from the temptation to sin. Rather, it means that the penalty for your sins has been paid once for all, and that your *position* is perfect before God. However, if you sin, your *condition* before him is that of a disobedient child who has broken happy communion with the Father in heaven. What is needed then is "parental forgiveness" from God as your loving Father.

The following discussion explains what happens to Christians when they sin, and how they can receive forgiveness and be restored to fellowship with God, their Father:

IF A CHRISTIAN SINS, THEN WHAT?

1. What has been lost?

a. *Not salvation.* Many young believers in Christ are haunted by the fear that their sins following conversion have robbed them of their salvation. This is one of Satan's most subtle wiles. Is it your experience? What does God's Word teach in this regard?

When a person trusts in Jesus Christ, he or she becomes a child of God: "For you are all the children of God by faith in Christ Jesus" (Galatians 3:26). Although a son may not always please his father, he is still a son. Likewise, although our behavior as children of God may not always be pleasing to our heavenly Father, we cannot annul this basic relationship. We are children of God by faith in Christ Jesus.

Notice also the words of the Lord Jesus. "I give unto

them [believers in Christ] eternal life; and they shall never perish" (John 10:28). When we believed in the Lord Jesus Christ, we received eternal life; as children we are heirs of eternal life through Jesus Christ (Galatians 4:7; John 3:16). This relationship to God can never change.

But perhaps you keep asking: "Then what have I lost since I was saved? I'm not happy in my Christian experience any more." Let John give you the answer:

b. *Fellowship with the Lord.* John, the disciple of the Lord Jesus Christ, wrote the epistle of 1 John to believers, so their joy might be full. (See 1 John 1:4.) Following the statement of purpose in his letter, the apostle wrote: "This then is the message which we have heard of him, and declare unto you: that God is light, and in him is no darkness at all. If we say that we have fellowship with him, and walk in darkness, we lie, and do not do the truth" (1 John 1:5–6). John is simply stating here that a person cannot sin (walk in darkness) and at the same time enjoy fellowship or communion with the Lord. (Notice Peter's experience in this matter, as recorded in Matthew 26:74–75.)

What then does the sinning Christian need to do?

a. *Confess sin.* John, writing under the guidance of God, wrote further: "If we confess our sins, he is faithful and just to forgive us our sins, and to cleanse us from all unrighteousness" (1 John 1:9).

When we confess our sins to God, we tell him the very sins we have committed. He knows what our sins are, but our confession is our honest acknowledgment to him of our personal sins. Notice that the verse says, "If we confess our sins . . . " It implies that confession should be specific. There is value therefore in mentioning particular sins before the Lord. Our part is to confess; it is his part to forgive.

b. *Forsake sin.* The Scriptures show how this involves putting sin to death and seeking things that are above: "If you then be risen with Christ, seek those things which are above, where Christ sits on the right hand of God. . . . Mortify [that is, put to death] therefore your members which are upon the earth" (Colossians 3:1, 5). Sincere confession of our sins leads to the forsaking of our sin (Proverbs 28:13).

c. *Make restitution.* If we have sinned against our fellow men, we have a responsibility to make good any loss, damage, or injury. Notice how Zacchaeus made restitution after meeting the Lord Jesus. (See Luke 19:8.)

3. What does the Christian receive when he or she confesses sin?

a. *Forgiveness and cleansing.* Remember that 1 John 1:9 tells us: "If we confess our sins, he is faithful and just to forgive us our sins, and to cleanse us from all unrighteousness." When we confess our wrongdoing, our loving Father forgives and cleanses us.

b. *Restoration of fellowship.* Note also the fellowship spoken of in 1 John 1:7: "If we walk in the light, as he is in the light, we have fellowship one with another, and the blood of Jesus Christ his Son cleanses us from all sin." Having confessed our sins to God, we are walking in the light again, enjoying fellowship or communion with him.

c. *Joy of victory over sin.* The Lord Jesus told his followers: "All things, whatever you shall ask in prayer, believing, you will receive" (Matthew 21:22). When we confess our sins and ask forgiveness, we receive this forgiveness. We have joy because we know that "we are more than conquerors through him that loved us" (Romans 8:37).

Even as we received salvation by faith in Jesus Christ, so we also receive forgiveness, cleansing, restoration of fellowship, and the joy of victory over our sins when we confess them to God and by faith believe that he has forgiven and cleansed us.

The following wise counsel comes from Dr. Northcote Deck:

> We need to keep clearly in our minds the difference between our relationship with God as a Judge, and with God as our Father. At conversion, we are "born again," born into the family of God, and become sons of God. However we may behave afterward cannot alter or annul this basic relationship. The son of a father cannot now be unborn. He may disgrace his father but he is still a son by birth. And the same is true of our relationship with God. Thus by faith in Christ and his atoning sacrifice, we are forgiven once for all, judicially, by God as a Judge. But in our daily walk we may grieve our Father, and then the promise in 1 John 1:9 (the whole epistle is written to believers, "born ones") becomes needful and must be used: "If we confess our sins, he is faithful and just to forgive us our sins."

Why do we need forgiveness of sins—we who are once for all forgiven by God as a Judge? Because we have grieved our Father. The divine union is unaffected, but the communion has been interrupted; and we need "parental forgiveness" from God as our loving Father.

3

The Christian's Purpose in Life

"Your will be done" (Matthew 6:10).

What is your purpose in life as a Christian? In this chapter you will consider this question along with ways that will help you achieve this purpose.

LIFE PURPOSE IN RELATION TO GOD

Why is there a sunrise? Does it just happen that the earth goes around the sun? Or is it all a part of God's great purpose and plan? The daily sunrise is as unchanging as the laws that govern its action. For us it is a spectacle for continual wonder and awe.

We know from the Bible that both sun and earth had

their origin in the plan and purpose of God. He who is the Creator of the universe is also its Sustainer, ever fulfilling his eternal purpose. (See Psalm 19:1–6.)

So it is that you, as a Christian, are a part of God's eternal plan and purpose. That new life in you, begotten by the Spirit of God, is given to you so that you can respond to God's love with obedience and bring honor and glory to his name. You can realize this only as you are conformed to his will for you.

> The whole purpose of God for character is to make us like Jesus Christ. He is interested in . . . [seeing] the life of his beloved son reproduced in us by the indwelling of his Spirit.[1]

(See Romans 8:29, 12:1–2; 2 Corinthians 3:18; 1 John 3:2.)

LIFE PURPOSE IN RELATION TO MAN

The young Christian often asks: "What is my goal in life? Am I to continue in my old ways of getting all I can for myself? Or am I supposed to give everything to God, now that I am his child, and live in dependence upon him?"

These questions are self-centered rather than God-centered. The right question to ask yourself is this: "What is God's purpose for me in the world?" When you sincerely seek the answer to this question, you have the correct approach for an understanding of your purpose in life.

---

1   Alan Redpath, *Getting to Know the Will of God* (Downers Grove, Ill.: InterVarsity Christian Fellowship, 1954), p. 3.

1. To witness for Christ

A first purpose for the Christian in this life is that of being a witness for the crucified and risen Lord. (See Acts 1:8.) This is true because believers in Christ are a spiritual light in a dark world (Philippians 2:15).

Our message is one of condemnation and salvation at the same time—condemnation to those who reject the only redeemer, salvation to all who will receive him. (See John 3:16–21.) Because of the very nature of the message of the Gospel, believers are under *obligation* to bear it to all the world; for people are saved by the preaching of the Gospel, and people hear by the preaching of the Word of God (Romans 10:13–17). As John R. W. Stott has expressed it, "Every Christian is called to be a witness for Christ in the particular environment in which God has placed him."[2] And D. L. Moody once said, "There is no greater honor than to be the instrument in God's hands of leading one person out of the kingdom of Satan into the glorious light of heaven."

2. To live by God's standards

We must keep in mind God's standards of right and wrong. They are absolute while ours are relative to our situation, desires, and needs. We think of ourselves first, and regard God as an afterthought. Yet God is Creator and Sovereign. As his followers, we should yield all things to his control. We are to set our affection (mind) on things above, denying to self the wicked and ungodly evils of this present world (Colossians 3:1–17).

---

2 John R.W. Stott, *Personal Evangelism* (Downers Grove, Ill.: InterVarsity Press), p. 4.

3. To live by God's power

The purpose of the believer in this life is to practice the wisdom of God; for though it seems like foolishness to us, this wisdom is a part of a great and wise plan given by God himself.

Paul practiced the wisdom of God, even as he said in 1 Corinthians 2:2–5: "For I determined not to know any thing among you, save Jesus Christ, and him crucified. And I was with you in weakness, and in fear, and in much trembling. And my speech and my preaching were not with enticing words of man's wisdom, but in demonstration of the Spirit and of power: that your faith should not stand in the wisdom of men, but in the power of God."

This purpose is contrary to the ways of mankind, but it is pleasing in God's sight and soul-satisfying to his redeemed. Someone has well said, "I would not stoop to be a king after having the high privilege of preaching the Gospel of Christ."

How to Achieve Your Life Purpose

So far you have seen that the Christian's high purpose in this life is to please God in all things. Nothing else can take its place. To aim for less is to miss that which God intended for you. How then is his purpose for you in this life to be achieved?

This section is not a complete answer to this question; rather, it will show you how the remaining chapters of this book will help you achieve God's purpose for your life.

Three important areas are covered: personal habits

helpful to growth in the Christian life; how to live in the world as a witness to the Lord Jesus and as a victor over the forces of evil; and the importance of the church and the fellowship that it provides with other believers.

1. Daily quiet time with God

Many Christians have found that a daily time for communing with God in Bible reading and prayer provides necessary food for their spiritual growth. We shall call this the quiet time. This book will guide you in developing three important parts of your quiet time—Bible reading, prayer, and Scripture memorization.

a. *Bible reading.* A vital part of the communion with God each day is the time spent with his Word. During the earthly life of our Lord, he showed the importance of the Scriptures by the way he used them to defeat Satan and expose wicked hearts. @EX = His often repeated words, "'It is written,' are a declaration of the fact that he stood within the circle of the will of God . . . What that will permitted, he willed to do; and what that will made no provision for, he willed to do without.' [3]

b. *Prayer.* "If authority were needed for observing an early morning Quiet Time, the writings and example of men of God in all ages would supply it. But the example of our Master himself, who, 'rising up a great while before day . . . went out, and departed into a solitary place, and there prayed,' is sufficient evidence of its supreme importance for us."[4] (See Mark 1:35.)

---

3 G. Campbell Morgan, *The Crises of the Christ* (London: Pickering & Inglis, Ltd.), p. 121.
4 Frank Houghton et al., *Quiet Time* (Downers Grove, Ill.:

c. *Scripture memorization.* As the Lord Jesus breathed the very air of Scripture, so our hearts and minds should be filled with memorized passages, made our very own during our quiet time. When we hide God's Word in our hearts, it can guide us and be ready for instant use. "You cannot stand in these days against the power of evil unless you are feeding your soul and your mind and heart with the Book. 'Man shall not live by bread alone, but by every word that proceeds out of the mouth of God' (Matthew 4:4)."[5]

2. Victory in the world

The accomplishment of the Christian's purpose with respect to the world is made possible only as the believer keeps "looking unto Jesus" (Hebrews 12:1–2). He is first of all the Savior, but he is also the perfect example for the child of God. Though he was in the world, he was not bound by it. He was in it, but above it. He did not allow anything to hinder him from accomplishing his heavenly mission. He lived for a kingdom which was not of this world. He defeated all powers and the temptations of this world. Now, as his followers, we must occupy the same relative position in the world, by the power of the indwelling Holy Spirit.

Central in the earthly life of the Lord Jesus was his absolute obedience to the Father. Everything he did in this life was focused on that basic purpose. He came to give eternal life to sinners. He came to seek and to save the lost. He came to die. He was not distracted from his

---

InterVarsity Christian Fellowship, 1945), p. 1.

5   Alan Redpath, *ibid.*, p. 16.

purpose by any human deception or innovation. He was not defeated in his purpose by the opposition of the priests and other religious leaders of that day. He was not turned aside by the cunning deceit of Satan. His whole life was in perfect accord with the plan laid down for him in the eternal counsels of the Holy Trinity, before the foundation of the world. (See Ephesians 3:11.)

> The Lord Jesus Christ never permitted one rival claim to God's will. Because he never permitted a rival claim, God led him, directed him, guided him, and brought him through to victory.[6]

What an example for every believer who wants to do the will of God!

3. The fellowship of the Church

There is yet other help available in achieving our life purpose as Christians, and that help is found in fellowship with other believers. The members of the local church, as one family, called "the household of God" (Ephesians 2:19), help one another. Theirs is a practical oneness in Christ that fosters growth in every area of the Christian life.

The church also provides opportunity for Christians to identify themselves with the Lord Jesus in baptism, and to remember him and proclaim his death by sharing with other believers in the Lord's Supper.

The remaining chapters will show how the three areas just discussed can be a part of your daily experi-

---

6   *Ibid.*, p. 9.

ence, helping you to know and to fulfill your purpose in life.

Don't be discouraged at the big task ahead. Growing as a Christian is like making a cable; we weave a thread of it every day, and every day its strength increases.

4

How to Read the Bible

"When he, the Spirit of truth, comes, he will guide you into all truth" (John 16:13).

The Christian life is a walk with Christ. The Lord Jesus is the constant Companion of the believer. He points the way in times of decision. He restores the soul when sin is confessed. He gives wisdom and strength in times of discouragement. He fills the life of his child with his joy as he has fellowship with his own (John 15:11; 1 John 1:3).

This walk with Christ can be a daily experience as the Christian spends time in the presence of the Lord. Bible reading and prayer are a practical means of a daily meeting with God at a definite time, and of fellowship with him at all times. Through his Word he speaks to his children according to their needs and gives them food for their soul. Through prayer the believing heart responds and is blessed.

It pleases the Father that we, his redeemed children, go to him in love and worship. He wants us to go to him of our own free will and out of love to him. He desires our fellowship. (See John 4:23.) Surely the fact that he wants our fellowship should make us want to spend time in his presence every day!

WHY READ THE BIBLE?

Whether we are "newborns in Christ," or have been his children for many years, we cannot give our best to him in devotion or service without daily food for our souls. We need the Bible every step of the way—from regeneration to glorification.

Here are some ways in which God's Word helps us:

1. For correction

The Word of God is necessary for spiritual correction. Paul wrote to Timothy saying, "All scripture is given by inspiration of God, and is profitable for doctrine, for reproof, for correction, for instruction in righteousness" (2 Timothy 3:16). Nothing can search out the secret sins and cleanse the heart as the Word of God can. Reading Scripture will often lead us to confess our sin and seek the forgiveness of Christ. The psalmist expressed it like this: "How shall a young man cleanse his way? By taking heed to your word. . . . Your word have I hid in my heart, that I might not sin against you" (Psalm 119:9, 11).

2. For counsel

Life is not a bed of roses. Besides the many temptations to do evil, we are faced with all kinds of practical problems. How we respond to them is a test of our Christian growth. The psalmist told us the secret of such growth and how he trusted in the counsels of the Lord to keep him in the center of his will. This is what he said to God: "You will guide me with your counsel, and afterward receive me to glory" (Psalm 73:24).

3. For warfare

The key to Christ's victory over the temptations of Satan in the wilderness was his dependence on God's Word. He used the power available to any person who is obedient to the Father's will; he applied the Scripture which had been written by Moses under the guidance of the Holy Spirit.

When properly used, as Christ used it, the Word of God is the Christian's armor, as well as his effective sword. How vital it is then for the believer to spend time daily in God's presence through the reading of his Word! (Study our Lord's example as recorded in Matthew 4:1–11.)

4. To know God

Scripture shows us what God is like in all his greatness and majesty, and reading the Bible shows us the various aspects of his wisdom and power as the Creator and Sustainer of all things. Reading intensively day by day will help us appreciate more fully the greatness of salvation in Christ; it will teach us of his love.

PREPARATION FOR READING THE BIBLE

There are certain practical requirements to keep in mind that will make Bible reading more effective.

1. A quiet place

A quiet place for unhurried and uninterrupted study and meditation is almost a necessity. Usually it is possible to find a quiet room or corner in which to read and pray without too much distraction. This may be your bedroom, living room, kitchen, or some other quiet retreat. Do not wait for an ideal location, but resolve to meet God daily somewhere.

2. A definite time

Even more important than a definite place is a definite time for daily Bible reading. Many people find that fifteen minutes to an hour in the early morning is best. Establish this habit now. Keep your quiet time with the Lord Jesus, despite the circumstances. If you should miss a day, don't give up, but continue in faith. Satan, who well knows the power of the Scriptures, will do his best to make it impossible for you to keep a regular time for Bible reading. Set a time and guard it jealously.

3. A spirit of expectancy

Above all, you should come to your time alone with God with an air of expectancy. Make it your objective to meet Christ personally. Believe him, that he will give you food for your soul. Trust him for a promise to claim. Ask him to show you any sin in your life and to cleanse you, so that you may enjoy the fellowship of his presence.

Before you begin reading your Bible, make the following verse the prayer of your heart: "Open my eyes, that I may behold wondrous things out of your law" (Psalm 119:18).

4. A Bible and a notebook

Get a good Bible with readable print and wide margins that allow space for notes. A notebook in which you can record what a specific passage means to you personally is valuable for future reference and study. Some have found it helpful to write in complete sentences, and in the first person, something like this: "Today I learned . . . "

The various editions of the *Bible Study Notebook* and the *Weekly Prayer and Study Journal* offer helpful guidelines for your spiritual journaling.

ACTUAL READING OF THE BIBLE

To help give proper direction to your Bible reading, a devotional guide is included in the back of this book.

Here are some suggestions to follow as you use it.

1. Read with a purpose

While we may read the Bible very rapidly in a survey course to learn all the facts, and very thoroughly in an analysis course to find the deeper meaning, these are not the purposes in devotional Bible reading. In devotional reading we should let God speak to us personally. Because of this, most people find it best to read only a short passage during the quiet time, to find out what God has for them.

Many like to read only as much as is needed to give a

unified thought. Sometimes this may be a verse or a paragraph, while at other times it may cover a whole chapter or more. When we read too much, we may get lost in the passage and miss its spiritual application to our own lives. The daily readings in the devotional guide are very short and are selected for their key thought. Watch for it.

2. Read thoughtfully

Reading only a short portion allows us to be more deliberate in thinking through the exact meaning of every phrase and sentence. God's Word is alive and speaks powerfully if we will give it time to sink. This requires the diligent application of our mind to the Scriptures, to seek out every possible meaning and application.

AFTER READING, APPLY THE WORD

In our quiet time we should think God's thoughts after him. His truth will be fixed in our minds as we express it by means of prayer (as we shall see in the next chapter), or as we write it down in our notebooks. Some days we will want to memorize a key verse that has been of particular blessing to us.

Seek daily to tell another Christian what God has given you. Use the results of your quiet time to tell others about the Lord Jesus. This will add vitality and freshness to your Christian life.

BIBLE READING GUIDES

After you complete the devotional guide, you know

how guides for daily Bible reading can be a definite help to Christians.

You may want to continue with the well-known plan of The Scripture Union, which takes you through the Bible in five years, with selected readings and pertinent questions for meditation and study.[1]

There are also simple calendars of readings that take readers through the Bible in one year. Young Christians, however, may find that they cover too much ground in too short a time with the one-year plan. Experience will help you decide this matter.

The *Weekly Prayer and Study Journal*, mentioned earlier, offers several plans to read the Bible through in a year.

If one plan of Bible reading does not meet your need, change to another. The possibilities are limitless! And you will want to select the plan you like best.

DEVOTIONAL BOOKS? YES OR NO?

There are devotional books that have Bible verses arranged in topics for each day of the year. These are good, but they are not a substitute for the Bible. There are also daily devotional books, written by devout Christians, with meditations for each day of the year. While good in themselves, at best they are only a supplement to daily Bible reading and ought never to replace it.

In all your effort, get deep into the Scriptures, for

---

1   *Daily Bread*. Order from The Scripture Union, 1885 Clements Road, Unit 226, Pickering, Ontario L1W 3V4. A nominal fee is charged.

through them God will speak to you by his Holy Spirit. While you read the Bible to master it, in the end it is much more important that the Bible master you. It is all-important that you see in it the portrayal of your living Lord and his will for your life.

5

*H*ow to *Pray*

"The effectual fervent prayer of a righteous man avails much" (James 5:16).

Prayer, in addition to Bible reading, is vital to the success of the Christian life because of our need to commune with God. Therefore, in this chapter we see what prayer is and what is necessary for effective prayer.

WHAT IS PRAYER?

1. Communion with God

Augustine said, "Prayer is our speech to God." A common conception is that prayer is merely asking things of God. But it has a deeper meaning than just asking. It is "directed conversation," "talking with a purpose." It is far more than mere conversation with another human being; it is talking with God!

2. An attitude of heart

Prayer has many aspects—worship; thankfulness; praise; expressions of love, confession, and submission; petitions or requests of God.

The Lord's Prayer is an excellent pattern for us to study and follow. Note the various aspects of this prayer as shown here: "Our Father, who is in heaven [an expression of love and dependence]. Holy is your name [worship]. Your kingdom come. Your will be done in earth as it is in heaven [submission]. Give us this day our daily bread [request]. And forgive us our debts, as we forgive our debtors [confession]. And lead us not into temptation, but deliver us from evil [request]: for yours is the kingdom, and the power, and the glory, forever [praise]. Amen" (Matthew 6:9–13).

Prayer is communion with God. Not only is it God's gracious provision for our peace and joy; it is also necessary for Christian experience. But why?

WHY PRAYER IS NECESSARY

Christianity is more than Bible truth to believe; it is a life to be lived! And that life finds its expression in following Jesus, listening to his voice, and obeying his instruction. He who has spoken to us through his Word wants to hear our response. And we need to unburden our hearts to him. For this reason, prayer is more essential to the Christian life than communication between close friends.

What purpose, then, does prayer serve?

1. As an expression of faith

Prayer is the means whereby we express our faith in God. By it we invite him to enter our lives, perhaps in the words of the publican's prayer, "God be merciful to me a sinner" (Luke 18:13). On the contrary, if we have no desire to pray, it may be that we have never received new life in Christ. And if a believer in the Lord Jesus is prayerless, he or she evidently has unconfessed sin because the neglect of prayer is sin (Luke 18:1). Yes, prayer is a necessary expression of faith.

2. For conformity to God's will

Prayer conforms us to the will of God so that our wills respond to what he wants for our lives. We are made sensitive to his will as we spend time reading and meditating on the Word of God and in praying about its message. As we pray, we are awakened to our true spiritual condition of mind and heart; for then God exposes our motives and desires, whether good or bad. Because prayer is that which he uses to bring our outlook into conformity with his perfect plan, we find that he realigns our thinking about the problems we face, problems for which we are asking his help. Prayer will remake; yet not prayer, but the God to whom we pray.

3. As a source of power with God

We must pray, not only because of the effect upon us, but also because through prayer we are asking God to intervene in life situations. We all have problems that are too much for human wisdom and power, but through prayer we may be linked with the eternal God, and with him "all things are possible" (Matthew 19:26).

"Effectual, fervent prayer" in the quiet time is spiritual labor, but it is also a source of power with God. By it we may see him work in our lives—the Supernatural controlling and directing the natural. Through prayer we have the privilege of participating in the work of the Lord around the world and in the lives of our friends. Through prayer we may see God hold back the forces of evil pitted against the lives and work of his servants.

One believer described prayer as the way to *renew* our human power, *release* heaven's power, and *resist* Satan's power. The rewards to earnest prayer are immeasurable; and there is no limit to God's power.

Sometimes we hear people say, "I do pray, but God doesn't seem to answer." That remark leads us to consider certain conditions we must meet if we want to prevail in prayer.

REQUIREMENTS FOR PRAYER

The requirements for prayer are similar to those for Bible reading:

1. Reverence and humility

Because God is holy and all-powerful, and because we are sinful and limited in knowledge and power, we must go to him in reverence and humility. Pride in any form will hinder prayer and mar our fellowship with our Lord. Christ himself showed us the empty hypocrisy of the Pharisee's prayer. (See Luke 18:9–14.)

2. Faith in God

We must go to God in prayer expectantly, as well as with reverence and humility. If he is all-powerful, and he is, then surely he wants to meet our needs. "The prayer of the upright is his delight. . . . He hears the prayer of the righteous" (Proverbs 15:8, 29). An honest, sincere faith that God will answer is the spirit that should characterize all of our prayer life.

The Savior wants us to trust him. He told Jairus, whose little girl had died, "Be not afraid; only believe" (Mark 5:36). His word to a father with a demon-possessed son was, "If you can believe, all things are possible to him that believes" (Mark 9:23).

3. Submission to God's will

Yieldedness to God's will follows faith. God is sovereign, and our lives should always be in submission to his perfect will. He wants to act on our behalf in the wisest way. Sometimes our asking is restricted because of our narrow view of things. But our all-knowing God sees what lies ahead, knows what is best, and will act accordingly. Therefore, if we are sometimes disappointed in the answers to our prayers, we should still thank God for his wise choice in the matter, remembering that "all things work together for good to them that love God" (Romans 8:28). This attitude of expectancy and faith cannot help but give peace of mind and joyfulness of spirit.

Now having met these requirements, at least in some measure—always, only, by God's grace—you may still ask, "But *how* shall I pray?"

How to pray

Generally it is best to spend time in prayer after reading the Bible, for then God has been speaking to your heart. You are open to spiritual thoughts, and your mind and heart have been prepared for prayer.

1. How should we address God in prayer?

Since our God is the Holy Trinity—three persons in one God—how should we address him in prayer? What does the Bible say about this? The answer is not hard to find.

Normally we pray to the Father in the name of the Son in the power of the Holy Spirit. This seems to be the Scriptural pattern. (See, for example, John 14:13; Matthew 6:9.) It is not wrong to address each person of the Godhead, especially in worship and thanksgiving; for, remember, the three persons are one God.

Your prayer may take the form of confession, praise, or petition, depending upon your special need, or upon the message God has given you from the Bible.

2. Worship and praise in prayer

You will find it helpful to begin prayer in your quiet time in a reverent spirit of worship, speaking to your heavenly Father of his greatness, majesty, love, and grace. Along with worship, offer your praise and thanksgiving as you recall his guidance and goodness in your life. Thank him for his work in the lives of others. Certainly there is much for which to thank and praise him (Hebrews 13:15; Psalm 10:3).

3. Confession in prayer

Out of your worship and thanksgiving will come confession of sin. This was the experience of Daniel who, in his prayer recorded in Daniel 9:4–14, did not spend all of his time asking, but worshiped God and confessed his own unworthiness and the sins of his people.

Confession of sin is necessary for all of us if we want to pray effectively, for God must cleanse our hearts and renew the power of his Spirit within us before he can hear and answer our prayers (Psalm 51:16–17).

4. For what should we ask?

Is it right to pray for just anything? Should we pray about little details of our daily routine? Yes, "nothing is too great for his power; nothing is too small for his love." He invites us to share the most minute details of our lives with him.

On the other hand, as we grow in prayer and fellowship with God, our circle of prayer interest will become larger, and prayer for those about us will become more and more important to us. This is what God wants. (See 1 Timothy 2:1-2; Ephesians 6:18–20; James 5:16; 2 Corinthians 1:11.) Do the teachings of these verses suggest a pattern for your prayer life?

5. The practice of prayer is not easy

We are likely to lead an ineffective prayer life because of a lack of discipline; therefore, we would do well to take the advice of older Christians who lead a successful prayer life. Here are a few suggestions:

a. *A prayer list.* Write in a notebook the names of the people for whom you would pray and the problems and projects in which you are interested. This helps you keep them before your mind and to pray for them regularly. It is easy to forget even the items that are close to our hearts. But don't be bound to a prayer list. Sometimes the Holy Spirit will lead you into prayer apart from it. Be sensitive to his leading so that your prayer does not become mechanical.

b. *Posture in prayer.* Is it necessary to kneel while praying? This question is often asked. Examples of kneeling, sitting, standing, or lying prostrate on the ground before God—all are given in the Bible (2 Samuel 7:18; Ezra 10:1; Psalm 95:6; Luke 18:13). It is beneficial to kneel if we intend this position to be a sign of our submission to the Lord. But kneeling beside a bed or a soft chair may encourage drowsiness. It is far better to stand and be alert than to kneel and go to sleep. Obviously the attitude of the heart is more important than the posture of the body.

c. *Aloud or silently?* Praying aloud often helps you give expression to prayer and keeps your mind from wandering.

d. *Continuing the spirit of prayer.* If you have been diligent in setting aside a quiet time for reading the Bible and praying in the morning, you will find that it is easy to speak to God in prayer during the day. Remember, you need not speak audibly; you may pray silently.

This was the experience of Nehemiah, the cupbearer for King Artaxerxes, whose practice it was to pray for his people and his country. On one occasion he prayed to God even before he attempted to answer a question asked by the king (Nehemiah 2:4). His prayer must have been silent and very brief, but he prayed.

6. Hindrances to prayer

There are many obstacles to successful prayer. But they can be overcome by God's grace and our own diligence. Here are some of the chief obstacles to successful prayer:

a. *Unconfessed sin.* Sin that is not confessed immediately

cripples our effectiveness. This makes it necessary for us to be sensitive to sin, shunning it always; and if we do slip into it, to confess it immediately (Psalm 66:18).

b. *An unforgiving spirit.* The Lord Jesus told us that an unforgiving spirit hinders prayer. There is no answer to this but to confess the sin to God, and if necessary to correct the situation with the person involved (Matthew 5:23–24).

c. *An undisciplined life.* Satan's most effective weapon in hindering us from prayer is an undisciplined life. An overcrowded schedule, late hours, irregular habits—all crowd out prayer. We must determine by God's help to regulate our lives so that a certain time each day is spent in prayer. This is a stringent demand, for it is very easy to pamper ourselves. But if we are to live for God and enjoy his blessing, we must deny ourselves and set aside a definite time for Bible reading and prayer.

7. Conclusion

Prayer, then, is communion with God. Each day, after he has spoken to you through the reading of the Bible in your quiet time, you should spend time speaking to him in prayer.

Worship and praise him.

Confess your sins and unworthiness.

Present your request.

Claim his promises in faith (1 John 5:14–15).

Go forward believing that God has heard and will answer.

6

*H*ow to Witness

"You shall be witnesses unto me" (Acts 1:8).

Ten men were gathered in a room to recall recent events and to talk about how some of those who loved the Lord Jesus had seen him in his resurrection body.

Their Savior and Lord had been taken away from them. They remembered his sinless life and the times of blessing and fellowship they had had with him for about three years. And now, while they were yet speaking about his death and resurrection, he appeared in their midst. Amazed, the disciples realized at once that the Lord they loved was really back with them.

Then the risen Christ explained to them from the Old Testament Scriptures how it had been foretold that he should "suffer, and . . . rise from the dead on the third day: and that repentance and remission of sins should be preached in his name among all nations, beginning at Jerusalem." And he added, "You are witnesses of these things." (See Luke 24:46–48; compare with Acts 1:8.) These disciples had *seen* the crucified and risen Lord!

YOUR MESSAGE AS A WITNESS

The message of Christianity is the story of the Son of God who suffered, died, and rose again from the dead on the third day, bringing remission of sin to all who repent and believe in him. The early apostles saw Christ in person—his life, death, and glorified resurrection body. They were witnesses with a message to preach to the whole world! Despite threats and persecution, they continued telling the story of salvation because, as Peter and John said: "We cannot but speak the things which we have seen and heard" (Acts 4:20).

Likewise, we today can speak as witnesses for Christ on the basis of a personal experience with the living Lord. Our witness will continue to be effective only as long as we stay in a right relationship with him.

WHY YOU SHOULD WITNESS

The urgency of a clear witness for Christ stems from the fact that people are saved by hearing the Word of God (Romans 10:17). And from whom shall they hear it except from those who know it and have obeyed it? What was perhaps the last command of Christ to his disciples still stands: "Go therefore, and teach all nations, baptizing them in the name of the Father, and of the Son, and of the Holy Spirit: teaching them to observe all the things I have commanded you: and be assured, I am with you always, even unto the end of the world" (Matthew 28:19–20).

Love's greatest gift of all time is the salvation God gave to us in Christ Jesus. He sent his only Son, who was dearest to his heart, and offered him up as our substitute. His righteous nature demanded that sin be punished; and apart from his Son there was no other sinless sacrifice. No other being was infinite and absolutely holy, and therefore able to pay the price of redemption.

Moreover, God desired that we should respond to his love. Such love knows no cost, and it can be answered only with love that flows out to others and shares with them this great salvation. Therefore, as we tell others about Christ, we do it in obedience to his command, but much more as a response to his love which has reached out to us and brought us in to the very presence of God. Such love must be shared.

YOU CANNOT HELP BUT WITNESS

Every Christian is a witness for the Lord Jesus, whether we will it or not. The light received by faith is like the city set on a hill; it cannot be hid. This does not mean that every follower of Christ must be fluent in talking about him. It simply means that every believer will in some manner reveal the new life within. As a result we cannot help but witness for the Lord!

Because of a testimony that honored God, Paul could say to the Thessalonians: "For our gospel came not unto you in word only, but also in power, and in the Holy Spirit, and in much assurance; as you know what manner of men we were among you for your sake" (1 Thessalonians 1:5).

A further evidence of Paul's effective witness for Christ is seen in his imprisonment with Silas at Philippi. Even as stocks and bars held them fast, they sang hymns of praise to God. When an earthquake freed them, they did not flee. The jailer, who would have killed himself, was stopped by Paul's assurance that no prisoners had fled. He was so convicted that he could only cry out, "What must I do to be saved?" (Acts 16:30).

What if we were persecuted as Paul and Silas were? Would the testimony of our lives be such that it would convict someone who is not saved?

QUALIFICATION OF A WITNESS

1. A surrendered life

The first need of an effective witness for Christ is a surrendered life. Your message as a Christian witness is not your own but God's. Therefore, his Lordship in this vital area of life must be recognized. The fact that you represent him and not yourself makes doubly important the kind of life you lead. People around you will watch you closely to find out whether you seek to serve your own interest or the Lord's. It is only as we give ourselves fully to the will of the Lord Jesus that we can serve him with our highest devotion; for the very nobility of this high calling is that of an ambassador: "Now then we are ambassadors for Christ, as though God did beseech you by us: we pray you in Christ's stead, be reconciled to God" (2 Corinthians 5:20).

2. Christian love

In addition to the self-surrender needed to serve the

best interests of the Lord whom we represent, there must be a deep interest in and a real love for those among whom we live. Love seeks out the best in a person and strives to develop it to the fullest extent.

The best and finest in a person is his or her soul. God made us in his own image and likeness; and though we are marred by sin, we can be changed by the redemption that is in Christ Jesus and given a glory far greater than that of the Garden of Eden. "Beloved, now are we the sons of God, and it does not yet appear what we shall be: but we know that, when he shall appear, we shall be like him; for we shall see him as he is" (1 John 3:2).

God alone can regenerate a human's soul and transform it into a thing of glory for his name. But ours is the privilege and responsibility of telling others of this grace. The Lord Jesus valued our souls so highly that he gave his life for our redemption. Do we value the souls of those about us enough to show them our love for Christ's sake?

We may not be called upon to show love for others by dying for them; certainly even such self-sacrifice could not redeem their souls. But we can manifest our love by dying to ourselves—denying personal convenience and advantage, so that we may be able to show kindness to someone else. Christ said that he would honor even a cup of cold water given in his name!

Such acts of kindness do not excuse us from the further responsibility of witnessing for Christ to those with whom we come in contact for a short time, or even once. However, they do stress the need for consistency and constancy in the witness of our daily lives for our Lord.

Requirements of a Witness

Love for the lost is shown through four characteristics of a good Christian witness: prayer, persistence, adaptability, and Bible study.

1. Prayer

The first step to be taken by the believer who wants to witness for Christ is to seek God's wisdom and power. This access to God may be our privilege as we pray to him in our quiet time daily. There we may speak to the Savior about those to whom we would witness and ask the Holy Spirit to work in their hearts. Thus the one we want to reach for Christ is prepared for the message of the Gospel. And there will be results! The psalmist wrote of effects of a soul-winner's godly concern and earnest prayer, saying: "He that goes forth and weeps, bearing precious seed, shall doubtless come again with rejoicing, bringing his sheaves with him" (Psalm 126:6).

2. Persistence

True Christian love for others is demonstrated by persistence. Yes, persistence! Many a time you may witness to a friend about Christ, only to be rebuffed. Will you be patient enough to realize that God has his hand in your sincere desire to lead souls to him? At still other times you may talk to someone who recognizes the need of the Savior but does not want to accept him just then. Will you persist in prayer and witnessing and let God do his work in his time? Your persistence will be tried in all ways and at many times; but with the love of Christ in your heart, there will always be enough patience too.

3. Adaptability

Zeal for Christ is tested by adaptability. One who wants to reach people for God must become "all things to all men," that he may win some. (Compare 1 Corinthians 9:19–22.) No two people are alike, and each one must be treated as an individual.

However, there are underlying principles that may be applied to everyone. This can be done with skill and discernment by one who loves the Lord Jesus, has studied the Bible, and has asked God for help in witnessing for Christ.

4. Bibly study

The message is God's and not our own. If that is to be so in fact as well as in theory, we must study his Word to know it as we ought. The Word of God has the promise of his blessing (Isaiah 55:11). Our own words are fleeting and transient. God's Word is alive and will endure forever. Surely that is the message we would give as ambassadors for the King of kings.

No doubt you have already discovered in your daily Bible reading that some verse or passage seemed to meet your particular spiritual need. Bible reading in the quiet time should also help you in witnessing to others and in answering the questions that arise in the course of your contact with people.

This is only one phase of Bible study, however; we also need the teaching ministry of a local church, Bible study books, and other Christians.

HOW TO WITNESS

In your witnessing you will find it helpful, first of all, to have a genuine interest in individuals and their needs. Usually people will give serious thought to our message only after they believe in you as a friend they can trust. Many who have accepted Christ as Savior testify to this.

1. How to approach the unsaved

a. *With kindness.* Kindness, freely given for Jesus' sake, is powerful. Think of the people who went out of their way to befriend you. To remember them is always a pleasure. Should it not be said of us too, as followers of our Lord, "Christians are the finest people I know; they always go out of their way to be kind"?

b. *With personal interest.* To be an effective witness for Christ you forget, for the time being, your own little world and enter into the problems of others. You may not know all the answers to their questions, but the giving of yourself to share in their problems will be richly repaid. People will soon find out whether your love is genuine, and not a mere interest for personal advantage.

c. *With hospitality.* Hospitality is almost a lost art in this modern, materialistic age. To share of yourself will take time and cost money. The question is, "Shall I spend it on myself, or shall I invest it for the sake of the Lord Jesus?"

Not every Christian can preach or do some public ministry, but all of us can invite a neighbor for a meal or for a cup of coffee and, in the course of conversation, share what Christ has done for us. There need be nothing forced about it. For example, you may explain that you read the Scriptures in your home at mealtime.

Invite your guest to listen as you read and let the Bible speak for itself.

d. *In dependence on the Lord.* The message of the Gospel must penetrate the heart before it can do its effective, life-changing work. The love of Christ must flow in you and through you to those who do not know him.

His love for the lost cost him everything he had. Because of it, he was willing to lay aside the glory of his heavenly home, to live among sinners. He became Man and bore the punishment for sin which was not his own. In a measure, that is the kind of love you must have if you want to win people to Christ. It means in practice that you must enter the lives of others, by sympathy and imagination, to see life from their standpoint; and by loving concern impress upon them the necessity of being born again. This can be done, not in your own strength, but in the power of the risen Christ living in you. Claim that power by faith!

2. What to tell the unsaved

In witnessing for the Lord Jesus we must use the Word of God because only it can clearly present the fact of sin, the work of Christ on the cross, and the necessity of the new birth. In a brief summary, here are these truths. Explain them clearly from the Scripture to the one you are seeking to win for Christ.

a. *The fact of sin.* Sin as a personal and present reality must be acknowledged. Every person has sinned and falls short of the glory of God (Romans 3:23). The effect of sin is death, both physical death and separation from God. That is the just payment for sin, whereas God's salvation is a free gift (Romans 6:23). As unrepentant sinners, we are dead in our sin and can do nothing to save ourselves

(Ephesians 2:1, 8–9; Titus 3:5). We need a Savior to bring us to God!

b. *The meaning of the Cross.* While we were still in our sins, God loved us so much that he gave Christ to die for us (Romans 5:8). He paid for our sins on the cross (Isaiah 53:5–6). The curse of the law, which was on us (Galatians 3:10), was laid on him (Galatians 3:13). Christ, the innocent one, suffered in our stead, that we might go free (1 Peter 3:18).

c. *The need of conversion.* To recognize the *fact* of sin and the *provision* of salvation does not make us a Christian. A definite step of faith is necessary, by which we put our trust in Christ as Savior. Only "whoever believes in him" shall "not perish, but have everlasting life" (John 3:16). Only those who "receive him" become the "sons of God" (John 1:12). There is no other way by which we can be saved (Acts 4:12). "You must be born again," the Savior said (John 3:7). "Come now, and let us reason together, says the Lord: though your sins be as scarlet, they shall be white as snow; though they be red like crimson, they shall be as wool" (Isaiah 1:18).

Now is the time to begin to witness. You may feel inadequate but just begin telling what you know. Notice the witness of the blind man who had just been given his sight. When questioned about his experience, he answered: "Whether he [Jesus] is a sinner or not, I don't know: one thing I know, that, whereas I was blind, now I see" (John 9:25).

OTHER MEANS OF WITNESSING

Besides the methods of personal witness for Christ, there are various public means of proclaiming his Gospel. One of the basic methods is that of preaching or teaching. This can be done in churches, missions, halls, or wherever people gather. Most Christians can easily distribute tracts and Gospel literature. Visiting those in hospitals, institutions, and at home can be most profitable. Many groups of Christians have street meetings that result in great blessing to themselves and other believers as well as in the salvation of souls.

Again, it must be remembered that in all witnessing for Christ certain basic principles are ever true:

1. We may *lead* people to Christ, but he *saves* them.

2. The best witness for Christ is a *word* for him, supported by a consistent life.

7

*S*cripture Memorization

"Your word have I hid in my heart" (Psalm 119:11).

A young Christian and one who had walked with Christ for many years were sharing what God had given them in their daily quiet time with the Bible and prayer. As they talked, the young believer observed that, while he spoke about a passage in vague terms, his companion frequently quoted a verse from the same passage, referring to it in a specific manner.

"Tell me," asked the young Christian, "why is it that you can often quote a verse from the passage that we're talking about and explain so clearly what it teaches?"

"It's just this," answered the older believer, "I make it a regular part of my quiet time to memorize a key verse that has been of particular blessing to me. Then I have something to take with me through the day, as well as a key to help me remember the passage in the future."

WHY MEMORIZE SCRIPTURE?

The Bible message spoken to you in your quiet time will go with you into your daily life and make it a potent spiritual force. When thus applied, the positive results of God's Word in your life will be growth, victory over temptation, cleansing from sin, and true wisdom.

Again, Scripture hidden in the heart will be readily available for future use in our witnessing for Christ. The use of Scripture in soul-winning is necessary because it is God's Word. No person is saved apart from the power of the Spirit of God and according to the Word of God (John 6:63). This is true because the Spirit of God uses the Word of God to convict of sin, to show how one can be born again, to give assurance of eternal life, and to teach the believer how to live for Christ. He who wants to win people to the Lord Jesus cannot possibly do it without the Word of God.

WHERE TO BEGIN

1. Choose a key verse from your Bible reading

No doubt you have already discovered that the Bible is an inexhaustible mine of spiritual wealth. Daily we can come away from it with our cups filled to overflowing. Yet we cannot be content with merely filling the cup; we must drink of it to get its spiritual benefit. The prophet Jeremiah said: "Your words were found, and I did eat them; and your word was unto me the joy and rejoicing of my heart" (Jeremiah 15:16).

2. Choose a key verse from the lesson you are studying

A key verse on Scripture memorizing is found in Psalm 119:11. There, as in many of the Psalms, each verse is often such a gem that we forget the setting in which it stands. This may have happened with Psalm 119:11: "Your word have I hid in my heart, that I might not sin against you."

Examine the whole stanza in which the verse is found. What is the setting? Does it deal only with the learning of Scripture passages by memory? The answer is no! It really shows us how a young man is looking for guidance from the Word of God for cleansing from sin in his life. It shows us how this young man will apply the truth expressed in the preceding verse. And in the rest of the stanza we find him praising the Lord for his goodness and his law.

Here we have two illustrations of the secret of making a passage live: we master it as a whole concept, and then memorize a key verse in the passage. The rest of this chapter will show you how to memorize such verses.

HOW TO CONTINUE MEMORIZATION

For your first memory verse I suggest either Romans 12:1–2 or Psalm 119:11.

Other suggested memory verses are printed on pages 111–114. They can be easily cut out into small cards.

Many people who memorize Scripture regularly find

verse cards convenient for use in learning as well as in reviewing in spare moments. When you wish to add new verses to your list, prepare cards of the same size. Write the verse on one side and the references on the other.

1. Make the verse meaningful

A first step in good memory work is that of making the verse meaningful. For this you need to know the context from which it is taken. If you memorized Romans 12:1–2 and Psalm 119:11 as suggested earlier, do you know how these verses fit into their chapters? Is the reason they were written clear in your mind? If not, go back and review the process until these verses live for you.

A memory passage must live for you, not only in its context, but also in terms of your experience. Ask yourself this question, "How does this verse apply to my life?" This will help you associate it with your needs and make it a part of your own experience.

2. Read—Recite—Review

Now, with a clear understanding of what the verse means, take the card and read the entire passage several times. Consider all of its main thoughts until you are familiar with it. Then read it over until you can say it without looking at the card. Carry the card with you during the day and review it in your spare time. You should go over it daily for at least six weeks in your quiet time or during spare moments.

MEMORY WORK MUST BE SYSTEMATIC

To establish your Scripture memorization on a systematic basis, try to learn one Scripture verse for each of the remaining chapters of this book. If you already know the suggested verses, learn one of the alternates.

Of the two suggested verses for each succeeding chapter, one is related to the devotional guide and the other is related to the particular chapter.

REVIEW—REVIEW—REVIEW

Because we forget quickly, we need intensive review at the beginning of the learning process. A new verse should be recited daily for at least six weeks, then once a week for six months, and periodically after that if it is to be firmly fixed in mind.

The secret of successful memorization of Scripture lies much more in effective and systematic review than in mass learning of new verses. Remember: learn the new verses well; but never neglect those already learned, lest they be lost to you.

REVIEW WITH A NEW VIEW

It is likely that you will find the daily review of verses already learned not quite as challenging as memorizing new ones. Yet this need not be so when you review them in response to one of these four questions:

1. *How does this verse fit into the chapter?*

Remembering the answer to this question will teach you both the verse itself and the truth of the whole passage.

2. *What other verses are similar to this one?*

This will show you how to compare the teachings of various Bible portions.

3. What do I know of a given Bible book from the verses I've learned?

Thinking about memory verses in this light will help you grasp the general content of a specific book without recourse to outlines or notes.

4. *How can I use this verse?*

Viewed in this light, the memory selection will become practical. We learn best when we relate the Bible to our own lives and experiences.

Use these four questions, or others you may discover, to help you vary your method of reviewing verses you have memorized.

8

The Christian's Warfare

"Put on the whole armor of God . . ." (Ephesians 6:11).

"Sure I'm a Christian. There's no doubt about that, but I wonder about this conflict inside of myself. Sometimes it seems as if the old urge to live high, to want to see and do things that may not be right, and to dream about being a great success is just as strong as before I was saved. Is this right for a Christian? I thought it would be much easier to live for Christ after I gave my life to him—or was I mistaken?"

THERE'S A WAR ON!

What you are saying is the experience of many, but

71

lct's look at it this way. We know that there are forces for good and forces for evil. In the Christian life we soon realize the power of these forces over us. There is within us the same *old*, strong desire to please ourselves; and there's a *new*, more noble, desire to do that which is right and pleases God.

You will find this internal tug of war explained in Galatians 5:17, which says: "For the flesh lusts against the Spirit, and the Spirit against the flesh: and these are contrary the one to the other: so that you cannot do the things that you would."

Behind the desires of the flesh are Satan and his hosts, while in the Spirit we have the power of God. There is therefore a conflict in our souls between the forces of light and the forces of darkness.

In this conflict you have a vital role as a participant. You chose sides at the time you trusted Christ as your Lord and Savior. Now you are a soldier in the cause of Christ, and dedicated to accomplish his purposes in this world.

1. The nature of the warfare

This is not a battle against mere people who may oppose the Gospel of Christ. As you will find in Ephesians 6:12, "We wrestle not against flesh and blood [people], but against principalities, against powers, against the rulers of the darkness of this world, against spiritual wickedness in high places." In this warfare we do not fight to gain merit with God, because all of our merit with him is in Christ. We do fight Satan and his hosts because they try to hinder and defeat God's purposes in this world.

James 4 describes the battleground in this fierce conflict. What does it tell us? The first verse gives the location of the battlefield: "in your members." Then it is no wonder that we are almost torn apart with desires to do good and almost equally strong desires for evil. The incorrigibly wicked old nature is not removed at conversion, but is still within us wanting to do that which is not pleasing to God; whereas our new nature, under the leadership of the Holy Spirit, is seeking to please God.

The reality of this conflict is felt in the life of every believer through temptation to sin. It is true that Satan uses various methods of temptation to attack the children of God in this world. But he ever seeks to induce the Christian to go beyond the bounds set by God, either through disobedience or through the improper use of things good in themselves.

2. The two opponents

To get a good perspective of the battle, we must understand the nature of God and Satan, the opponents. God is holy and pure. God is light. Nothing evil, impure, or unholy clouds his character. His very presence dispels darkness. Thus God's Spirit at work in the life of the believer, through the new nature, produces that which seeks to please God and shun evil.

Satan is the very incarnation of evil. This once-beautiful angel rebelled against God and was cast out from his position of honor and glory (Isaiah 14:12–15; Ezekiel 28:12–19). From that day to this, his unceasing objective has been to bring dishonor upon, and to destroy, the work of God. The old nature, or our natural self, can still be influenced by Satan and his hosts. The world system by which we are constantly influenced is under the domination of Satan.

HOW SATAN ATTACKS

The spiritual conflict in which we are all engaged comes to us in temptation. Thus Satan, the god of this world, makes his appeal for us to do evil by going beyond bounds set by God. The apostle John, in his instructions to young Christians, gave a stern warning against loving the things of this world, even as he described the nature of Satan's attacks: "Love not the world, neither the things that are in the world. If any man love the world, the love of the Father is not in him. For all that is in the world, the lust of the flesh, and the lust of the eyes, and the pride of life, is not of the Father, but is of the world" (1 John 2:15–16).

To help you obey this important command, 1 John 2:15–16 has been selected as a memory text for this chapter. This Scripture passage will remind you that, to live a godly life in this present world, you must deny the unrighteous, wicked lusts within you.

The phrases, "lust of the flesh," "lust of the eyes," and "pride of life," summarize Satan's areas of attack on the Christian, that is, how he tempts us. To be forewarned of this ever present danger, let us examine these sources of temptation in detail.

1. "The lust of the flesh"

This is the avenue of approach Satan uses to make us go beyond the bounds of proper physical appetites. We can yield to the lust of the flesh by impurity of life, intemperance, and self-indulgence.

The basically impure mind of mankind is seen in Galatians 5:19 and Romans 1:24–28. For a Christian to yield to immorality, described in these passages, is to bring dishonor to Christ and to invite God's judgment (Galatians 6:7).

Intemperance, or overindulgence in food and drink, is another way to grant the desires of our physical appetite in the wrong way. Thus even the necessities of life can become a hindrance instead of a help.

Self-indulgence becomes a snare in a land of ease and plenty, a land that is loaded with "creature comforts." Soft springs can make sleep too easy for those who want an excuse to avoid Bible reading each morning. Automobiles and too-ready facilities for amusement can quickly rob us of time that should be used for God and others. Are "creature comforts" to be our masters or our servants?

We are forcefully reminded in 1 Corinthians 6:19–20 that the believer's body is "the temple of the Holy Spirit." Dare we defile it by impurity or intemperance? Dare we do less than let God fulfill in us the noble purpose for which he made these bodies of ours and bought at such a price?

2. "The lust of the eyes"

Through our eyes we see things in this world and are attracted to them. Our eyes should serve a useful purpose, as God intended; and we should not use them to satisfy our lustful and covetous nature.

In his direct and forthright manner Christ said: "Whoever looks on a woman to lust after her has committed adultery with her already in his heart" (Matthew 5:28).

The Lord Jesus was stressing here the sinfulness of impure thoughts, which begin with the lust of the eyes. Appeals of this nature are continually being made in pictures, books, magazines, movies, and television, which often boldly display the so-called "glamour type." Yet, while we may successfully resist such blatant appeals, we may much more easily yield to impure thoughts at the sight of some physical attractiveness. Or we may think unduly about beautiful clothes or a new car. We must be careful even with the proper desires of life.

Not only are we tempted through the eyes to indulge in impure or improper thoughts, but we are also tempted to covet things that are good in themselves. During Israel's battle with Jericho, Achan saw a beautiful Babylonian garment and some gold and silver. Immediately he coveted them and took them home to his tent, in disobedience of God's command that everything in that city should be destroyed. This sin, which resulted in Israel's great defeat at Ai, was punished by the death of Achan and his family (Joshua 7:20–26).

The lust of the eyes is also to be seen in the temptation of Eve in the Garden of Eden. She saw that the forbidden fruit was desirable because it was pleasant to the eyes. But the eating of that fruit was evil because it was beyond the bounds set by God.

3. "The pride of life"

"I am better than anyone. I can do things better than anybody else. I like the achievements I have gained for myself. I like the position I hold. I only wish I were a bit further up the scale. I like the possessions I have. I only wish I had more." Are we guilty of such thoughts? What does all this mean? Nothing less than pride—that sin which caused the downfall of Satan. Even today it is a powerful tool that he uses in temptation. And this is how he does it:

a. *Personal vanity.* This is a human weakness. Satan attacks it with telling blows. Vanity because of personal appearance, real or imagined wisdom, ability, or skill—personal vanity in all of its varied expressions—has caused many to fall. But God's Word says: "When you correct man for iniquity you make his beauty to consume away like a moth: surely every man is vanity" (Psalm 39:11). "He that glories, let him glory in the Lord . . . for what do you have that you did not receive?" (1 Corinthians 1:31, 4:7).

b. *Pride of achievement.* Nebuchadnezzar, king of ancient Babylon, lifted up his heart in pride one day as he looked at the beautiful city he had built. He asked himself: "Is not this great Babylon, that I have built for the house of the kingdom by the might of my power, and for the honor of my majesty?" (Daniel 4:30). In "the same hour" his kingdom was taken away from him and the deposed king was driven out to live among the beasts and birds of the field for seven years. Restoration came, but only after he had humbled himself and acknowledged the God of heaven.

As Christians, we must say, with Paul: "By the grace of God I am what I am" (1 Corinthians 15:10).

c. *Pride of position.* A place of position and prestige is desired by many people. It is their feeling that a place of influence and authority (even in the church!) will give them the means for accomplishing the things they dream about. Such was the appeal made to Eve in Eden when Satan told her that eating the forbidden fruit would make her "as gods [or, God], knowing good and evil" (Genesis 3:5). Adam and Eve soon realized the folly of their pride, but it was too late. The Scripture says, "Whoever exalts himself shall be abased; and he that humbles himself shall be exalted" (Luke 14:11).

d. *Pride of possessions.* Christ said that life does not

consist in the abundance of possessions. He illustrated this truth with the story of "the rich fool" who tore down his barns to build bigger ones and then died suddenly in his folly. "So is he that lays up treasure for himself, and is not rich toward God." (See Luke 12:13–21.)

Possessions, like the abilities, strength, and position that God has given us, are but a trust from him, for which we shall be held accountable. To have and to enjoy things pleases us and may make us well thought of by others. But what is our chief aim? Possessions can be used for the glory of God; but they are a snare from Satan if we pride ourselves in them.

WHEN A CHRISTIAN YIELDS TO TEMPTATION, WHAT HAPPENS?

Thus far we have seen that temptation comes to the believer in Christ through various appeals of Satan; and that these appeals may come singly, in various combinations, or all at once as they did to Adam and Eve. (See Genesis 3:1–7.) As it was in the first temptation, so it is also today: yielding brings sin into the life. In the unbeliever, sin is a barrier of separation from the presence of God. For the believer, sin breaks fellowship with God.

RESTORATION AFTER FALLING INTO TEMPTATION

The good hand of God on his child who has fallen in temptation leads the erring one back to the place of restoration. Confession will be necessary, but the child of God who is obedient will gladly confess his or her sin in order to be restored.

9

*H*ow to Meet *Temptation*

"Turn from your evil ways, and keep my commandments" (2 Kings 17:13).

As a follower of the Lord Jesus, you will inevitably meet temptation in this world; but in Christ you may have victory over it. When Satan comes with temptation, you can overcome him by claiming God's power and provision for deliverance. How the application of this provision and power can lead to victory over temptation is the subject of this chapter.

CLAIM YOUR POSITION IN CHRIST

Salvation in Christ is certain. It is as sure as the unchanging Word of God, which tells us how we are saved and how we may *know* that we are eternally secure in Christ Jesus. During times of testing and temptation we will be assailed by doubts and fears as to our standing before God. Yet, need we be afraid? The answer is an unqualified No!

Salvation is not of ourselves; it is provided by the redemptive work of Christ (Ephesians 1:7). It is our possession because we have believed on him (John 3:36). As this truth first assured us of the fact of our new birth, so it assures us also of our eternal standing in Christ. In him we are beyond the destructive power of the enemy (Romans 8:38–39). At the moment Satan tempts us with doubts about our salvation, and our security in the Lord Jesus, we should claim such promises as that found in 1 John 5:11–12: "And this is the record, that God has given to us eternal life, and this life is in his Son. He that has the Son has life; and he that has not the Son of God has not life".

WALK IN OBEDIENCE TO GOD AND HIS WORD

Although we are forever safe in Christ, all too often we grieve him by our disobedience. It is only when we are in the path of obedience, as revealed to us in God's Word, that we are kept by his power from yielding to temptation.

Many centuries ago the Holy Spirit spoke through Samuel the prophet, saying to the disobedient king Saul: "Has the LORD as great delight in burnt-offerings and sacrifices, as in obeying the voice of the Lord? Behold, to obey is better than sacrifice, and to listen is better than the fat of rams" (1 Samuel 15:22).

Today, as in the time of Samuel and Saul, solicitation to evil tempts us to go beyond the bounds set by God. He set these bounds for our protection and safety. For us to go outside of them is to wander into sin.

Scripture is forthright. It tells us what we should do and what we should not do: " . . . denying ungodliness and worldly lusts, we should live soberly, righteously, and godly in this present world" (Titus 2:12). To turn from the evils of this world to Christ, is to live in his light, where sin cannot abide. Obedience to God and his Word will strengthen us in the time of temptation because we are in fellowship with him, and have the assurance of his presence and power. "And whatever we ask, we receive of him, because we keep his commandments, and do those things that are pleasing in his sight" (1 John 3:22).

But perhaps you are thinking: "I know I'm forever secure in Christ, and I've dedicated my whole heart and life to him. But everywhere I turn I see and hear evil things. To be entirely frank, I am tempted. Is this a sin?" The Bible's answer is No. It is not a sin to be tempted. Our sinless Savior was tempted. It is sin to yield to temptation. Our Lord did not yield to Satan's wiles. And that brings us to another must:

ACTIVELY RESIST SATAN

James, that wise and practical leader in the early church, gives us this word about how to defeat Satan: "Resist the devil, and he will flee from you" (James 4:7).

We cannot do this in our own strength. We can do it only in the strength God has given us to fight the spiritual warfare in which we are engaged. Thus James says at the beginning of this same verse: "Submit yourselves therefore to God."

In Ephesians 6:11–17, Paul gives us a picture of God's provision for the believer's warfare, describing the Christian soldier's weapons and armor. Study the passage carefully to see that the loins are to be girt about with truth; the breastplate represents righteousness; the feet are to be shod with the preparation of the gospel of peace; the shield is faith; the helmet speaks of our salvation; the sword of the Spirit, our offensive weapon, is the Word of God. Thus we see that the believer is provided with the complete armor of God with which to face Satan and his attacks.

While there are times in which we must actively oppose Satan in battle, there are also times when we must resist him by fleeing from temptation as Joseph did from Potiphar's house. (See Genesis 39.) Temptation is too subtle and powerful for us to resist in our own strength. To play with it is to play with fire!

TRUST IN GOD'S KEEPING POWER

Satan is a strong enemy, but our God is all powerful. He has made provision for our victory over Satan by the power of the Holy Spirit who dwells in every believer in the Lord Jesus. To every Christian God says: "Your body is the temple of the Holy Spirit" (1 Corinthians 6:19). "Greater is he [that is, the Holy Spirit] that is in you, than he [that is, Satan] that is in the world" (1 John 4:4). "God . . . is able to guard you from stumbling" (Jude 24 ASV).

And how does he guard us in the hour of temptation? Study 1 John 5:1–5, which gives us the basis for claiming the victory that is ours in Christ: "This is the victory that overcomes the world, even our faith" (v. 4).

God's keeping power reaches right down to the actual temptation. He has promised that we shall be able to bear the testing, and that with it will come a way of escape. Here is a verse for this chapter that will give you the assurance of God's faithfulness to you in times of temptation: "No temptation has taken you but such as is common to man: but God is faithful, who will not permit you to be tempted above that you are able; but will with the temptation also make a way to escape, that you may be able to bear it" (1 Corinthians 10:13).

HELPS FOR OVERCOMING TEMPTATION

1. A daily quiet time

By now, the practice of time alone with God is doubtless a part of your daily schedule. In the previous chapters on Bible reading, prayer, and Scripture memorization, you saw the importance of this quiet time for your Christian life and growth. This chapter on temptation includes some questions that may help you to relate to your quiet time more specifically to the darts of the evil one:

a. *Bible reading.* Time spent in God's Word each day gives us the courage needed for spiritual strength. Are you depending upon the Scriptures for the guidance and insight necessary to meet temptation and the warfare against the forces of evil?

b. *Prayer.* Prayer is our response to God as he speaks to us through his Word. Are you exercising your great privilege of asking for wisdom to make right choices, so that you may withstand temptation?

c. *Scripture memorization.* Chapter 7 suggested a method of regular Scripture memorization. How have the verses you have learned so far been of help to you in your Christian life? Do you see any verses in this chapter that you want to memorize to help you overcome temptation?

Surely the power of the enemy and the subtilty of his attacks should make us watchful. We must always rely on God's Word to guide us and on his power to keep us. Spending time with him each day can help us do this.

2. A disciplined life

A positive step away from temptation is a disciplined life, which does not make room for the flesh and its yearnings for self-gratification. Here are a few suggestions:

a. *When to pray.* Set aside a definite time each day for Bible reading and prayer.

b. *Be steadfast.* Do not flinch or withdraw when serving the Lord may seem a hardship or an inconvenience.

c. *Honor God with your substance.* Be careful how you spend your money. You are responsible for it as a steward.

d. *Deny self.* Guard against feeding your mind on that which does not honor God. Starve the old nature, and feed the new nature by seeking those "things which are above" (Colossians 3:1–17). Follow the instructions given in Romans 6:11–13.

3. Christian fellowship

"If we walk in the light, as he [that is, God] is in the

light, we have fellowship one with another" (1 John 1:7).

There are many ways in which you may share in Christian fellowship. Here are some ways that will help you have victory over temptation:

a. *Choose the right kind of companions.* "Be not deceived: Evil companionships corrupt good morals" (1 Corinthians 15:33 ASV). Seek the companionship of fellow Christians at your school or place of employment and you will avoid many temptations. To spend your time profitably, you and these Christian friends might have an informal Bible study period, or you might review memory verses.

b. *Meet with other believers in a local church.* You need the teaching ministry of the church to help you grow. You need the opportunities the church offers for worship and service. In all these ways you may excercise your faith in Christ. Help other believers in practical ways, thus showing your love for them (Romans 12:9–10).

In chapters 8 and 9 we have seen how all Christians are engaged in a spiritual warfare. We have seen how Satan tempts us to go beyond the bounds set by God. Yet, while we must be careful because of Satan's attacks and power, we do not fear defeat. Our certain victory and hope are in Christ, who will keep us in the time of temptation. No power of evil in all the world need shake because we know this hope: "Greater is he that is in you, than he that is in the world" (1 John 4:4).

10

*T*he Church and You

"Not forsaking the assembling of ourselves together" (Hebrews 10:25).

They were a small group. Only about one hundred and twenty people were gathered in the upper room following the departure of their Lord for heaven (Acts 1:15).

Through the days that followed his ascension, the disciples remained in Jerusalem until the day of Pentecost. Then the Holy Spirit came upon the assembled group of Christians with "tongues like as of fire" and with an effect that shook the world.

Deeply religious Jews from all over the known world were in Jerusalem for the feast of Pentecost and heard the mighty works of God proclaimed in their own languages as the believers in the Lord Jesus spoke. Amazed and awe-struck, the people wondered what was happening among the small band of followers of Christ. Some said they were drunk; but those who would listen heard Peter preach with great boldness, power, and life-changing effect, as we see by this account: "Then they that gladly received his word were baptized: and the same day there were added unto them about three thousand souls. And they continued steadfastly in the apostles' doctrine and fellowship, and in breaking of bread, and in prayers" (Acts 2:41–42).

Thus the small group of believers multiplied and grew into a vigorous young church of about three thousand who were loyal to God and active for him.

CHARACTERISTICS OF THE EARLY CHURCH

The fervent devotion of the early church and their boldness in witnessing stand out noticeably in the book of Acts. To find out directly what it was that so vitally affected these believers, look up the Scripture passages mentioned in this chapter. As you study the characteristics of the members of the early church, note these facts about them:

1. They sensed the reality of God in their midst

God was given first place in their hearts. His Word was gladly received, and believers in Christ were baptized. They continued in fellowship, Bible study, the teachings of Jesus, prayer, and the breaking of bread. A godly fear came upon them all, and many wonders and signs were done by the apostles. (See Acts 2:41–47.)

2. They ministered to one another's needs

The love and unity of the early believers are shown by their unselfishness. The believers at Jerusalem shared their material goods according to their various needs, and no one suffered want (Acts 4:32–37).

3. They were consciously accountable to God for their conduct

The swift and sudden judgment upon Ananias and Sapphira made the whole church aware that sin had been committed, not against a group of people alone, but against a holy God who judges people's hearts (Acts 5:1–11).

4. They shared responsibility

As the church increased in numbers, the Grecian Jews murmured because their widows were neglected in the believers' care for the poor. To meet this need, this responsibility was given to deacons, so that the apostles might give themselves more fully to the teaching of the Word of God and to prayer (Acts 6:1–4).

5. They were a witnessing church

From the beginning, the believers at Jerusalem were faithful in witnessing for Christ. Persecution, such as the stoning of Stephen and the persistent opposition from Saul of Tarsus, only drove them to more active witnessing wherever they went (Acts 8:4).

6. They were a praying church

The early church "continued . . . in prayers" (Acts 2:42), and her leaders gave themselves to a ministry of prayer (Acts 6:4). On one occasion their faithfulness was rewarded by the deliverance of Peter from prison after the whole church had prayed for him (Acts 12:5); and this is just one of many examples of God's answer to their prayers.

HOW THE CHURCH GREW

When opposition became too fierce at Jerusalem, they fled to Judea and Samaria, preaching the Gospel wherever they went. The result was that groups of believers, or local churches, were established in many areas.

Philip, the evangelist, went to a city in Samaria and preached, with the result that many were saved (Acts 8:4–12). Peter was led by the Holy Spirit to preach to the Gentiles in the house of Cornelius, the centurion, in Caesarea. Other believers preached the Gospel in such faraway places as Phoenicia and Antioch. Even Paul, who had once been the bitter enemy of the Church, was converted and became a builder in the Church. By the time the Jewish opposition diminished, local churches were already well established in many places. "Then had the churches rest throughout all Judea and Galilee and Samaria, and were edified; and walking in the fear of the Lord, and in the comfort of the Holy Spirit, were multiplied" (Acts 9:31).

HOW THE CHURCH WAS TAUGHT
AND ESTABLISHED

In establishing the churches in the faith, the teaching ministry of godly men under the leading of the

Holy Spirit played a vital part. One such man was Barnabas, an early leader in the Church. With Paul he ministered the Word of God at Antioch for "a whole year" (Acts 11:26). Together they exhorted the believers in that great city to remain faithful to God with a steadfast purpose. This ministry bore rich fruit later on, when God used these well-taught Christians at Antioch to send Paul and Barnabas into wider fields of service for him (Acts 13).

In his later ministry Paul spent long periods of time with churches he had founded, instructing them in the Word of God and teaching them how to follow Christ. Such a ministry kept him at Corinth for a year and a half (Acts 18:11), and in Ephesus for over two years (Acts 19:8, 10). Yet Paul not only preached and taught the believers there; he also prayed for them continually. Even after he left a church, he remained actively interested in it, anxiously awaiting word from its members and writing letters of instruction and correction as the need demanded. These letters, or epistles, which Paul wrote under the leading of the Holy Spirit, have been preserved in our New Testament for our use and guidance today.

This brief glance at the records of the birth and growth of the early Church shows us something of God's purpose and will for her on earth—her mission, her message, her very life in Christ Jesus, the Lord.

Choosing a Church

Wherever you are in the world today you will very likely find a group of believers in Christ banded together in a local church. You will find that your common bond with them is your mutual love for Christ. It is in him that we are united, one body. Now the local church is but the visible symbol of the great host of believers who make up the whole Church—the Body of Christ (Colossians 1:24). Note that in 1 Corinthians 12:27 and Romans 12:5 we are called members of that Body. Therefore, we are to recognize our place in it.

In tracing the history of the early church, recorded in Acts 2, you have seen how fellowship in a local church naturally follows conversion. But you may be asking, "What kind of a church shall I join?" Or perhaps you are wondering, "How can I find such a group of believers for Christian fellowship?"

As you ask yourself these questions and seek God's guidance from the Bible and through prayer, the Holy Spirit himself will lead you in choosing a church (John 16:13; Romans 8:14). Remember that God's promise of Psalm 32:8 cannot be broken: "I will instruct you and teach you in the way which you should go: I will guide you with my eye."

How the church will help you

Here are some ways a local church or group of believers can help you:

1. In growth as a Christian

The church will help you grow as a Christian through the teaching ministry of the Word of God. The faithful proclaiming of doctrine and practical truth for daily living will establish you in your faith and prepare you for serving the Lord Jesus (Colossians 1:23; 2 Timothy 3:16). You need encouragement for growth. Note specifically how the believers at Antioch met to tell of the Lord's blessing (Acts 14:27). You need direction, as well as correction, in your growth as a Christian. The writer to the Hebrews shows how this is to be done by fellow believers who "consider one another to provoke unto love and to good works . . . exhorting one another" in the light of Christ's return (Hebrews 10:24–25; also notice 1 Corinthians 1:10 and Philippians 4:2).

2. In prayer

As Christians we are members of the body of Christ. Therefore, what affects one member affects all the others. Paul tells us in Galatians 6:2 that we are to bear one another's burdens. How can we do this better than in prayer for our mutual needs and problems? See the examples in Acts 12:5 and 21:5.

3. In true worship

"God is a spirit: and they that worship him must worship him in spirit and in truth" (John 4:24). In the fellowship of the church we meet with others to bring to God the praise of a pure heart (Hebrews 13:15). We can do this by thanking God for his goodness, reading the Scriptures, singing hymns, offering prayers, presenting our gifts, and observing the Lord's Supper.

4. In fellowship

The joy that springs out of fellowship among brothers and sisters in Christ is very real. As the risen Lord is exalted, there is a uniting of hearts, minds, hopes, and aims. Then our human differences lose their importance, and the joy of being laborers together with him reigns supreme.

Paul expressed this joy when he wrote to the Philippians, saying: "I thank my God upon every remembrance of you . . . for your fellowship in the gospel from the first day until now" (Philippians 1:3, 5).

Your place in the church

The church is not only the body of Christ; she is also his bride. One day she will be called to be with her heavenly Bridegroom forever.

The local group of believers with whom you have fellowship is a part of the bride of Christ which will be caught up to be with him in that day. Even as an earthly bride prepares for and awaits the coming of the bridegroom, so you may show your love to Christ and prepare for his return as you take your place with fellow believers in worship and service to God.

How a believer is to share in the fellowship of a local church is to be seen from these principles set forth in the New Testament:

1. By baptism and the Lord's Supper

The ordinance of baptism is a symbol of the believer's identification with Christ. It follows conversion in the example of the church at Jerusalem, where those who were saved were baptized, and they shared in the fellowship of the church (Acts 2:41–42).

The Lord's Supper is a time of remembering Christ in his atoning sacrifice for sin (Matthew 26:26–28; 1 Corinthians 11:23–26).

2. By regular attendance

Meeting with fellow believers is important. The

writer of Hebrews warns us against neglect in this matter: "not forsaking the assembling of ourselves together, as the manner of some is; but exhorting one another: and so much the more, as you see the day approaching" (Hebrews 10:25).

Because meeting with other believers is important and because we need to be reminded of this privilege, Hebrews 10:25 has been selected as one of the memory verses for this chapter.

3. By regular giving

The proper support of God's work takes specific and regular giving. Paul exhorted the Corinthian Christians to set aside a definite part of their income each week as a contribution for the saints (1 Corinthians 16:2). It is a great joy for the Christian to be able to share material blessings so that the needs of the Lord's servants and his work may be supplied (2 Corinthians 8:1–5).

4. By service

The church is a proper sphere of service for God. There we can use our ability and expend our energy for his glory. To provide for the ministry of the church, God has given each one of us special gifts and abilities with which we may serve him. Note how they differ, as indicated in Romans 12:3–8 and in Ephesians 4: 11–12. And note God's purpose in bestowing these gifts, that we as believers may be established in Christ and that the Gospel may be preached to those who are lost. Our responsibility is to do what God has given us to do (Ephesians 4:16; 1 Corinthians 12), and to perform it faithfully until our Lord's return (Luke 19:13).

5. By unity of mind and spirit

Singleness of mind and heart is necessary if the church is to function properly and smoothly. In all our actions we must seek to bring honor and glory to Christ who is our Head. To do this we must walk in lowliness of mind and with love for one another: "endeavoring to keep the unity of the Spirit in the bond of peace" (Ephesians 4:3; notice also Philippians 2:3).

With great simplicity and clarity the apostle Paul shows us how the many members are all united in the church as the body of Christ (1 Corinthians 12:12–27). He shows us how every believer is a vital though different member of the body and fulfills an essential function in God's plan. Therefore, as members of one body, we need the help and fellowship of other believers for worship and service for Christ. In turn, they need our help and fellowship in the ministry of the gifts and abilities that God has given us. Enjoy the blessing of this experience by being a part of a local church. As you do this, remember that God's ultimate purpose for those who are members of his body, the church, is that we might be presented to him as his bride, "holy and without blemish" (Ephesians 5:27).

11

Baptism and the Lord's Supper

"This do in remembrance of me" (1 Corinthians 11:24).

By two direct commands the Lord Jesus Christ established the two ordinances of the church: baptism and the Lord's Supper. Baptism indicates identification with Christ, while the Lord's Supper reminds believers of the Savior "till he comes" (1 Corinthians 11:25–26).

BAPTISM

1. Baptism in the early church

Following the death and resurrection of the Lord Jesus Christ, he appeared to the eleven disciples on a

97

mountain in Galilee and spoke to them, saying: "All power is given unto me in heaven and in earth. Go therefore, and teach all nations, baptizing them in the name of the Father, and of the Son, and of the Holy Spirit: teaching them to observe all things I have commanded you: and be assured, I am with you always, even unto the end of the world" (Matthew 28:18–20).

The first record of the fulfillment of this command is found in Acts 2, where we read that Peter preached Christ to those gathered at Jerusalem. It was the day of Pentecost; and devout Jews "out of every nation under heaven" heard the believers speak by the power of the Holy Spirit. As they heard Peter preach Christ: "they were pricked in their heart, and said unto Peter and to the rest of the apostles, 'Men and brethren, what shall we do?' Then Peter said unto them, 'Repent, and be baptized every one of you in the name of Jesus Christ for the remission of sins, and you shall receive the gift of the Holy Spirit. . . .' Then they that gladly received his word were baptized: and the same day there were added unto them about three thousand souls" (Acts 2:37–38, 41).

The history of the early church, as found in Acts, records other instances of baptism of those who repented and believed after hearing the message of salvation through Christ. (Notice Acts 8:12, 35–38; 9:4–5, 17–18; 10:47–48; 16:14–15.)

2. What does baptism mean?

In this chapter we have already seen how the Lord Jesus instructed his followers to go, teach all nations, and baptize them "in the name of the Father, and of the Son, and of the Holy Spirit." We have also seen how the early church obeyed this instruction from their Lord. Today, as in the early church, water baptism is also a privilege that every believer may share.

It is well to note that water baptism is outward, and is distinct from the baptism of the Holy Spirit. The baptism of the Holy Spirit, according to 1 Corinthians 12:13, takes place in every believer at the time of conversion.

Water baptism is an external and visible rite symbolizing an inner experience of the believer in relation to Jesus Christ. This inner experience includes:

a. *The believer's union with Christ.* "For you are all the children of God by faith in Christ Jesus. For as many of you as have been baptized into Christ have put on Christ" (Galatians 3:26–27; notice also Colossians 2:11–12).

To believers baptism is a sign and seal of their vital union with Jesus Christ.

b. *The removal of the believer's sins through Christ's death.* "Don't you know, that so many of us as were baptized into Jesus Christ were baptized into his death? Therefore we are buried with him by baptism into death: that like as Christ was raised up from the dead by the glory of the Father, even so we also should walk in newness of life. For if we have been planted together in the likeness of his death, we shall be also in the likeness of his resurrection" (Romans 6:3–5). To the believer, baptism symbolizes the removal of the penalty of sins through the blood of Christ.

c. *The believer's identification with Christ in the power and reality of his resurrection life.* Notice again Romans 6:3–5, which points out the believer's provisions for leading a victorious life.

d. *The Lordship of Jesus Christ in the believer.* "For as many of you as have been baptized into Christ have put on Christ" (Galatians 3:27). We have died to self and have "put on Christ."

Here is an entirely new way of life. There is a new direction: new management, a new authority. In Matthew 28:19 the Lord instructed his followers to baptize in the name of the Father, the Son, and the Holy Spirit; this implies that those being baptized were bought under the authority of the Father, the Son, and the Holy Spirit. You now belong to Another.

Water baptism, then, is an act that identifies a believer with Christ. Therefore, because we are thus identified with him, we should "seek those things which are above" (Colossians 3:1–3). But "the flesh is weak" (Matthew 26:41); and to keep the message of Calvary before us, God has given us the Lord's Supper.

THE LORD'S SUPPER

On the night of the Passover, the Savior and his disciples met in an upper room to commemorate the first Passover in Egypt (see Exodus 12). Having announced that one in their midst would betray him, Jesus instituted the ordinance by which he would be remembered after his death.

Of that solemn occasion we read: "And as they were eating, Jesus took bread, and blessed it, and broke it, and gave it to the disciples, and said, 'Take, eat; this is my body.' And he took the cup, and gave thanks, and gave it to them, saying, 'Drink all of it; for this is my blood of the new testament, which is shed for many for the remission of sins'" (Matthew 26:26–28).

Thus "Christ our passover" (1 Corinthians 5:7) tells us that he came to die, as "the Lamb of God, which takes away the sin of the world" (John 1:29)

1. The Lord's Supper in the church

"This do in remembrance of me," the Savior said (Luke 22:19; 1 Corinthians 11:25). Thus the Lord's Supper reminds us of Christ's death and is to be observed in memory of him until he comes again (1 Corinthians 11:26).

The early church obeyed the Lord's command, and kept this ordinance. (See Acts 2:42; 20:7.)

a. *It is a time of remembrance.* From these Scripture passages, we see that the Lord's Supper was intended as a time to remember Christ in his atoning sacrifice for sin. It helps us express our love and devotion to him, even as it reminds us of his love and sacrifice for us.

In the sacredness of this time of remembrance, our attention is fixed upon the person of Christ. As he is seen in the light of his redemptive work, we realize our dependence upon him as our Savior. We remember that he alone could pay the penalty of our sin before a holy God. We are stripped bare of ourselves as we contemplate his love for us on Calvary.

b. *It is a proclamation to the world.* Not only is the Lord's Supper a time of remembrance; it is also a proclamation of the Gospel to the world. It tells others that salvation can be had only through faith in the person and work of Christ. "For as often as you eat this bread, and drink this cup, you do show [proclaim] the Lord's death till he comes" (1 Corinthians 11:26).

c. *It is an expression of the unity of believers in Christ.* To partake of the bread and the cup is to signify oneness in him through visible and material symbols of a spiritual reality, and to know the joy of communion with God and with one another. Notice what 1 Corinthians 10:16–17 says in this regard: "The cup of blessing which we bless, is it not the communion of [participation in, ASV] the blood of Christ? The bread which we break, is it not the communion of [participation in, ASV] the body of Christ? For we being many are one bread, and one body: for we are all partakers of that one bread."

2. The Lord's Supper and the individual believer

To the believer the Lord's Supper is a memorial of our Savior "till he comes." To eat the bread is to be reminded of his body broken for us, and to partake of the cup, or wine, is to be reminded that "without shedding of blood is no remission" of sin (Hebrews 9:22).

Indeed, the Lord's Supper is meaningless if we fail to see in it the purpose of Christ's death and the miracle of our union with him.

3. Who may participate in the Lord's Supper?

To meet with fellow believers at the Lord's Table is the right and privilege of every Christian. The Lord's Supper is observed in local churches, in keeping with the command of Christ who instituted and ordained it and in whose merits we come. He is the host at this, his Table; and he desires that all who are redeemed should join him there. No higher invitation could be given, and no lesser command should keep us away.

To those who might question their right of access to the Lord's Table, Paul said: "Let a man examine himself, and so let him eat of that bread, and drink of that cup" (1 Corinthians 11:28).

Then the apostle warned that anyone who participated in the Lord's Supper in an unworthy manner did so with the promise of judgment (1 Corinthians 11:29–30).

"IF YOU LOVE ME, KEEP MY COMMANDMENTS"

Baptism and the Lord's Supper, the two ordinances of the church, commanded by Christ himself, are the believer's privilege and responsibility. To obey them is to show our love (John 14:15) for him and to let the world know of his redeeming grace and power.

12

Your Next Steps

"Let us go on" (Hebrews 6:1).

Like the seed that the farmer sows in the field, the Word of God is spread throughout the earth. Some of it falls by the wayside; some on stony ground; some among thorns; and some on good ground, where it springs into life and brings forth fruit (Matthew 13:3–9). If you have trusted the Lord Jesus as your personal Savior, the good seed of the Gospel has sprung up in your heart unto life eternal.

The roots of this spiritual life are firmly implanted in this word of assurance from Christ himself: "Very truthfully, I say unto you, he that hears my word, and believes on him that sent me, has everlasting life, and shall not come into condemnation; but is passed from death unto life" (John 5:24).

This is the new and blessed life which knows the joy

of sins forgiven and has the abiding peace of a clear conscience before God (Psalm 32:1).

Psalm 1:1–3 gives us the Holy Spirit's description of the walk of the godly person, who is likened to a tree: "Blessed is the man that walks not in the counsel of the ungodly, nor stands in the way of sinners, nor sits in the seat of the scornful. But his delight is in the law of the Lord; and in his law he meditates day and night. And he shall be like a tree planted by the rivers of water, that brings forth his fruit in his season; his leaf also shall not wither; and whatever he does shall prosper."

THE WINDS THAT BLOW

While Psalm 1 presents a picture of the believer's life, we must remember that growth for a tree is never easy. There are the steady winds which continually buffet the tree, and the sharp and sudden winds which strike with tempestuous fury. Yet the tree "planted by the rivers of water" stands, not weakened, but stronger for the test. How like the Christian who also faces the winds of opposition—the steady winds of continual opposition and the sharp blows of sudden temptation!

1. The steady winds

The steady winds of opposition will probably come to you in one or more of these various forms:

a. *By trouble in the quiet time.* A steady wind of opposition will be felt in your daily struggle to keep a quiet time when it seems like drudgery instead of the joyful time it should be. But don't give up! Look for something for which to praise God each day. Don't let a busy life deprive you of this time with the Lord. You may find it helpful to order The Scripture Union notes as suggested in Chapter 4, for additional help in your quiet time.

b. *Discouragement.* Christians are often discouraged as they realize that their lives are not what they desire them to be. Even the apostle Paul had great struggles, as he confessed: "For to will is present with me; but how to perform that which is good I find not" (Romans 7:18).

Yet Paul did not give up. He persisted in pressing on in the Christian race (Philippians 3:14). And so must we.

Regular study of God's Word will help make your life what it ought to be.

c. *Christians who are stumbling blocks.* Misunderstanding and difficulties will arise even among fellow believers. Yet we are commanded to love one another. We can show this love by bearing one another's burdens and by ministering to one another's needs. And we are to be known to the world by our love for one another. The Scripture says: "Be kindly affectioned one to another with brotherly love; in honor preferring one another" (Romans 12:10).

2. THE SUDDEN WINDS

Along with the steady winds that strengthen us by their very opposition, there are the sharp and sudden winds of temptation which severely try the Christian. They often come in these ways:

a. *Sudden opportunity to do evil.* James 4:1 tells us how we are often driven by our "pleasures that war in" our "members" (ASV). They drive us to seize every opportunity to get gain for ourselves, without thought of its harmful effect on us or on others. We can overcome these temptations as we heed the teaching of James 4:8: "Draw near to God, and he will draw near to you."

b. *Appeals to impure thoughts.* These attractions are even more insidious and treacherous than the outward appeals to do this or that. They sap our strength and spiritual vitality. We must repel them by filling our minds with the truth of God as revealed in his Word. We dare not yield to "the lust of the flesh" (1 John 2:16), lest the things of this world choke the good seed and make it unfruitful (Mark 4:19).

Often we look at a tree which has withstood severe testing by wind and storm and marvel at the strength of its trunk and branches. We admire what we see but may forget about the unseen roots below, which are thrust down deeper and deeper because of every passing wind. Thus it is that the wind which would oppose and test is the wind that strengthens and helps in growth!

THE TREE THAT STANDS

So far we have seen how the faithful seed of the Word planted in the human heart grows into the tree that stands against the strong winds of opposition and the sudden winds which test its strength.

Why is this so? Because the tree is rightly placed at the source of strength. It is not in the desert, with only the sun, the wind, and the sand; nor is it on a hill, far from and above its source of life. The strong tree is next to the river, from which it can draw its strength without fail and without regard for the season. Its leaf does not fade and its fruit appears in due season (Psalm 1:3–4).

This tree could no more stand apart from its foundation of life than could the Christian stand if separated from the source of life in Christ. An illustration of the

Christian's dependence upon Christ is seen in the fact that we are branches of "the true vine" (John 15:1–16). As we obey the Lord's exhortation, "Abide in me," our obedience will lead to continual and steady growth, which in turn will result in the bearing of fruit. Remember, to love Christ is to obey him.

This book has been written to help you establish firm roots in your Christian life and to guide you in beginning daily habits that are useful for continued growth. Remember, completing this book is just the beginning of your growth. Here are some suggestions for continued growth:

1. Continue a daily quiet time

Do not neglect your daily time for prayer, Bible reading, and Scripture memory work.

2. Join a local church

If you have not already done so, become part of a local church for fellowship with other believers.

3. Witness

Share the joy of your new life with others—believers and unbelievers.

4. Continue your study

Remember that the purpose of growth is to glorify God. Make Philippians 3:14 your desire: "I press toward the mark for the prize of the high calling of God in Christ Jesus."

Live as you would if you knew that the Lord Jesus Christ were coming today to take you to heaven (1 Thessalonians 4:16–17), but plan your growth as you would if you knew that he would not return for another fifty years. "The day of the Lord will come as a thief in the night." "Beloved, seeing that you look for such things, be diligent that you may be found of him in peace, without spot, and blameless. . . . But grow in grace, and in the knowledge of our Lord and Savior Jesus Christ. To him be glory both now and forever. Amen" (2 Peter 3:10, 14, 18).

Hebrews 10:25
Church
Chapter 10

Matthew 28:19–20
Baptism
Chapter 11

2 Peter 3:18
Your Next Steps
Chapter 12

Romans 12:1–2
Dedication
Chapter 7

Joshua 1:8
Meditation
Chapter 8

Joshua 24:15
Commitment
Chapter 9

Psalm 119:11
Memorizing
Chapter 7

1 John 2:15–16
Worldliness
Chapter 8

1 Corinthians 10:13
Temptation
Chapter 9

But grow in grace, and in the knowledge of our Lord and Saviour Jesus Christ. To him be glory both now and forever. Amen.

Go ye therefore, and teach all nations, baptizing them in the name of the Father, and of the Son, and of the Holy Ghost: teaching them to observe all things whatsoever I have commanded you: and, lo, I am with you alway, even unto the end of the world. Amen.

Not forsaking the assembling of ourselves together, as the manner of some is; but exhorting one another: and so much the more, as ye see the day approaching.

And if it seems evil unto you to serve the Lord, choose you this day whom you will serve; whether the gods which your fathers served that were on the other side of the flood, or the gods of the Amorites, in whose land ye dwell: but as for me and my house, we will serve the Lord.

This book of the law shall not depart out of thy mouth; but thou shalt meditate therein day and night, that thou mayest observe to do according to all that is written therein: for then thou shalt make thy way prosperous, and then thou shalt have good success.

I beseech you therefore, brethren, by the mercies of God, that ye present your bodies a living sacrifice, holy, acceptable unto God, which is your reasonable service. And be not conformed to this world: but be ye transformed by the renewing of your mind, that ye may prove what is that good, and

There hath no temptation taken you but such as is common to man: but God is faithful, who will not suffer you to be tempted above that ye are able; but will with the temptation also make a way to escape, that ye may be able to bear it.

Love not the world, neither the things that are in the world. If any man love the world, the love of the Father is not in him. For all that is in the world, the lust of the flesh, and the lust of the eyes, and the pride of life, is not of the Father, but of the world.

Thy word have I hid in mine heart, that I might not sin against thee.

James 2:10
WORKS

Matthew 21:22
PRAYER

Acts 4:12
SALVATION
Chapter 10

Ephesians 2:8–9
SALVATION

1 Peter 2:2
THE WORD

Acts 5:29
OBEDIENCE
Chapter 11

John 3:36
SALVATION

James 1:5
WISDOM

1 Peter 1:18–19
SALVATION
Chapter 12

He that believeth on the Son hath everlasting life: and he that believeth not the Son shall not see life; but the wrath of God abideth on him.

For by grace are ye saved through faith; and that not of yourselves: it is the gift of God: Not of works, lest any man should boast.

For whosoever shall keep the whole law, and yet offend in one point, he is guilty of all.

If any of you lack wisdom, let him ask of God, that giveth to all men liberally, and upbraideth not; and it shall be given him.

As newborn babes, desire the sincere milk of the word, that ye may grow thereby.

And all things, whatsoever ye shall ask in prayer, believing, ye shall receive.

Forasmuch as ye know that ye were not redeemed with corruptible things, as silver and gold, from your vain conversation received by tradition from your father; But with the precious blood of Christ, as of a lamb without blemish and without spot

Then Peter and the other apostles answered and said, We ought to obey God rather than men.

Neither is there salvation in any other: for there is no other name under heaven given among men, whereby we must be saved.

DEVOTIONAL GUIDE

This devotional guide was written by Anthony C. Capon of the Scripture Union to help you with your own regular Bible reading and prayer. The weekly topics parallel the studies in this book. Start now to have a daily quiet time, preferably first thing in the morning. Wait upon God through his Word and in prayer, using as your guide the following *Four Phase Method:*

PRAY

Before reading, pray that God will help you to understand and to receive his Word. The Scripture Union prayer is: "Open my eyes, that I may behold wondrous things out of your law, for Jesus Christ's sake, Amen" (Psalm 119:18).

READ

Read carefully the Bible passage for the day.

MEDITATE

Meditate on what you have read, asking yourself questions such as:

1. What is this passage basically about?

2. What does it reveal about God?—the Father, the Lord Jesus Christ, or the Holy Spirit?

3. What are its implications for me? Is there a command, a promise, or a warning? An example to follow or an error to avoid?

Record your findings in a notebook, then compare your notes with the daily comment from this *Devotional Guide*.

PRAY

Pray after reading, using the thoughts you have gained as the basis for your prayer.

Weeks 1 and 2—John Looks at Jesus Christ

"We beheld his glory . . . full of grace and truth." These words from John 1:14 sum up the message of the chapters from John's Gospel which we read the first two weeks. John shows us (a) *Christ's glory*. He was "the Word" which "became flesh, and dwelt among us" (1:14).

He was God, moving among men. But John also shows us (b) *Christ's grace*. He came not to destroy us, but to save us by his own blood shed on the cross.

Week 1

Sunday: John 1:1–5

Underline the three titles used here of Christ. (a) *The Word.* Hebrews 1:1–2 explains why Christ is given this name. The prophets of old and Christian preachers today *pass on* the Word; but Christ *is* the Word—God's Word to man. (b) *The Life.* When nothing but God existed, Christ had life! Every other life springs from him. So he alone can give eternal life. (c) *The Light.* He conquers the darkness of ignorance, sin, fear, death. Has this great light flooded your own heart?

Question: How can the Word at the same time be "God" and yet "with God" (v. 1)?

Monday: John 1:6–14

"Sent to bear witness." This sums up the work of John the Baptist. He did not talk about himself, but about Christ, who is worth talking about. (a) *How Christ came.* Verse 14 tells us (look for these things) who he was, what he did, where he lived, what we saw, what it was like, and what he came to bring. It makes verse 11 almost unbelievable, until we realize how many people do the same today. (b) *Why Christ came.* Read verses 12–13 again. Underline the words, "As many as received him . . . were born . . . of God."

Question: In what ways are you actively witnessing for the Lord Jesus Christ?

Tuesday: John 1:29–34

Notice two titles given to Christ by John the Baptist. (a) *"The Lamb of God"* (v. 29). This is "sacrificial" language, and takes us back to the story of the Passover, when a lamb was killed so a family might live. Read what the Lord said in Exodus 12:12. Christ died that we might live. (b) *"The Son of God"* (v. 34). He is not only the One who died; He is the One who lives. The end of verse 33 tells us what he can do for us.

Question: To whom does Jesus give the Holy Spirit (John 7:39)?

Wednesday: John 3:1–8

Find the verse which tells us that to be born again is absolutely *essential*—it is a "must." Notice how Christ describes the new birth in verse 5. There are two parts to it. (a) *"Born of water."* Ezekiel 36:25 tells us what this means. Without the cleansing away of the *old* there can never be the beginning of the *new.* (b) *"Born of the Spirit."* Look at Ezekiel 36:26–27 for the meaning. After cleansing the temple of my life, God fills it with his Spirit! It all happens the moment I receive Christ as Savior and Lord.

Questions: Are you sure you are "born again"? When did it happen?

Thursday: John 3:9–17

Read the story Christ referred to in verses 14–15 (Numbers 21:4–9). It is a type or foreshadowing of Jesus Christ. The people who had been bitten by the serpents had to do two things: (a) *Admit their need.* Only when they said, "We have sinned . . . against the Lord" did God heal them. (b) *Come in faith.* When they looked to the serpent of brass they were instantly healed. We have an even better promise from God than they had (John 3:15).

Questions: Can you repeat verse 16 from memory? Do *you* have eternal life? Answer yes or no.

Friday: John 4:1–14

A thirsty woman. Christ was physically thirsty, but the woman's spiritual thirst was far more serious. What is *your* thirst today? *A thirst for forgiveness?* The water that Christ gives is a cleansing water to wash your heart and your conscience clean. *A thirst for fellowship?* Christ will talk with you as he did with the woman and meet your need. *A thirst for power?* The water he will give you is "living" water; it is in fact the Spirit, through whom his own mighty deeds were done.

Question: What is the "thirst" of which you are most conscious? Read verse 14 and claim it in prayer.

Saturday: John 4:15–26

(a) *The sinful woman.* Yes, sin was her real trouble; for all spiritual thirst comes from *sin*. What was her particular sin (v. 18)? Christ knew that her sin had to be brought out and dealt with before her thirst could be quenched. (b) *The saving work.* "Salvation is of the Jews" (v. 22); it was the sinbearer himself with whom she was talking (v. 26). (c) *The spiritual worship.* Once sin is cleansed away, there is open access to God, and then we can worship him (v. 23).

Question: Is any sin hindering Christ from fully supplying your needs?

Week 2

Sunday: John 6:1–14

Once again we see people in need; this time the trouble is *hunger*. And once again we learn something of what Christ can do. (a) *The people are hungry.* Surely this is a picture of all mankind, hungry for something, yet not knowing where to find it (v. 5). Isn't it true that even with all the benefits of modern life there is still an

119

unsatisfied longing in our hearts? (b) *The people are fed.* The best that *human* ideas can give is "a little" (v. 7). In *Christ* we can have as much as we need (v. 11).

Question: Only Christ could provide the bread. What could the disciples do?

Monday: John 6:27–37

"The bread of life" (v. 35). It is infinitely better than any "bread" this world can offer (v. 27). (a) *It is free!* Note the word "give" in verse 27. Nothing to pay. Well, must we do some "work" for it (v. 28)? What's the answer (v. 29)? No *work*, just *faith*—believe it and accept it! (b) *It is final!* You will never be disappointed and have to look somewhere else, for you will never hunger again (v. 35). (c) *It is for all!* Or rather, *he* is for all, since Christ himself is the Bread. Verse 37 is one to memorize.

Question: Are you satisfied with Christ? If you are still "hungry," you need to get to know him better.

Tuesday: John 7:37–44

(a) *The offer.* "Drink!" (v. 37). Oh, how true it is that there is complete freedom from all the anxieties and strivings and dissatisfaction of non-Christians when they learn to rest in Christ and be satisfied in him. (b) *The condition.* "Come!" (v. 37). Come *once*, for the first time, renouncing all else and taking Christ into your heart. Come *daily* to refresh yourself with him. But there were so many who *would not* come (vv. 41, 44). (c) *The result.* Overflow to others (v. 38)! True enough, a satisfied soul cannot help communicating to those around it.

Question: Does Christ produce division today (v. 43)?

Wednesday: John 10:1–9

There are two wonderful pictures of Christ here. (a) *The Door* (vv. 7, 9). Notice in verse 9 the two things the sheep find when they use the right door: *safety* and *pasture*. In what way do we have these in Christ? He is the doorway to all God's blessings. Make sure you have entered in. (b) *The Shepherd* (v. 2). In verses 3–4, underline in one color everything that the Shepherd does, and in another color all that the sheep do. Apply each point to yourself.

Questions: How well do you know the Shepherd's voice? How closely are you following him?

Thursday: John 10:10–18

(a) *Who the Shepherd is.* In verse 10 the devil is called a thief. See what he seeks to do with our souls. How different is Christ, the Good Shepherd. He wants us *dear* to each other and *near* to him (v. 16). (b) *What the Shepherd has done.* Verses 11 and 17 tell us. In verse 12 the devil is the wolf. Christ fought against him at Calvary, and gave his life that we might be saved from Satan's clutches. (c) *What the Shepherd gives.* "Life . . . more abundantly!" (v. 10). In this world or the next, there is no life that is fuller or more joyous than the life of a Christian.

Question: Who ordered Christ to die for the sheep (v. 18)?

Friday: John 10:24–30

(a) *The double condemnation of the unbelievers.* They heard *his words* and "believed not" (vv. 24–25); now they see *his works* and still "believe not" (vv. 25–26).

They ignore the evidence of both their *ears* and their *eyes*. How do unbelievers do this today? (b) *The double security of the believers*. Notice how differently these respond. "My sheep hear . . . and they follow" (v. 27). Consider their twofold security: they are held firm, Christ says, by *"My hand"* and by *"My Father's hand"* (vv. 28–29).

Questions: To whom does Christ make the promises of verses 27–29? Who are his "sheep"?

Saturday: John 12:23–33

Two deaths are spoken of here: Christ's and ours. (a) *Christ's death*. Surely verse 24 means that if Christ had not died to redeem us, not one soul could have shared eternity with him. He would have abided "alone." Now look at verse 32: the door to eternity is open! Yes, Christ *came to die* (v. 27). (b) *Our death*. We too must die. Christ is not speaking of our literal death, but of a completely new attitude to life (v. 25). We must die to the love of ourselves, and live only for Christ and for others.

Question: Verse 24 was certainly true of Christ. How may it also be true of us?

*W*eek 3—*Powerful Christian Living*

It is all too easy for Christ to get pushed out of the center of a Christian's life. This week we read the letter to Colosse, which Paul wrote to the Christians there to warn against this danger. Christ is the central theme of the whole epistle. The key phrase is in 1:18: *"that in all things he might have the pre-eminence."* Make use of our readings this week to check that Christ is really supreme in every part of your life.

Sunday: Colossians 1:1–8

Life with Christ in Colosse. Paul thanks God for the Colossian Christians' walk with Jesus Christ. (a) *The beginning of it—"faith"* (v. 4). They began to be pleasing to God only when they exercised "faith in Christ Jesus." That was the day when their lives began to be fruitful (v. 6). (b) *The continuing of it—"love"* (v. 4). Love came *into* their hearts by the Spirit (v. 8) and went *out* "to all the saints," just as Paul's love went out to them. (c) *The end of it—"hope"* (v. 5). Their life was like a race toward a finishing post. Heaven is at the end of the road.

Question: What do you think "fruit" means (v. 6)?

Monday: Colossians 1:9–17

(a) *A great prayer.* Here is a fine pattern to follow in praying for ourselves and others. Paul prays that they may have *spiritual knowledge* (v. 9) to understand God's way; a *spiritual walk* (v. 10) to follow it faithfully; *spiritual strength* (v. 11) to live a godly life; and a *spiritual attitude* (v. 12) of thankfulness for their glorious salvation. (b) *A great salvation.* Notice what God has delivered us *from* and translated us *into* (v. 13). Something to be thankful for, indeed! How was it brought about (v. 14)?

Question: What proofs can you find in verses 15–17 of the deity of Jesus Christ?

Tuesday: Colossians 1:18–23

(a) *The person of Christ* (vv. 18–19). There is only one place that is suited for Jesus Christ, the place of pre-eminence (v. 18). "It pleased the Father" that it should be so, and nothing less can please us. Has he pre-eminence in *your* life? Anything less is unworthy of him. (b) *The work of Christ* (vv. 20–22). We have his work *in the past*—"the blood of his cross"; his work *in the present*—"and you . . . has he reconciled"; and his work *in the future*—"to present you holy . . . in his sight."

Question: There is a condition ("if . . .") in verse 23. How seriously are you taking it?

Wednesday: Colossians 2:1–7

(a) *Christ is the secret of sound thinking* (vv. 1–5). How much there is to learn before we come to "the full assurance of understanding" (v. 2)! And how easy it is to be led astray "with enticing words" (v. 4)! Only if our studying is Christ-centered can we be sure we are on the right track (v. 3). (b) *Christ is the secret of sound living* (vv. 6–7). Our living must be Christ-centered too. It must not be just an imitation of someone else's life, but a personal walk with Christ as Lord.

Question: Just how far does Christ enter into your daily thinking and daily living?

Thursday: Colossians 3:1–11

(a) *Up above!* Verses 1–4 show us Christ glorified in heaven; they say, in effect, "If he is your *treasure,* that is where your *heart* should be too!" Why allow our hearts to be enslaved by *"things on the earth"* if he is all our life? (b) *Down below!* One day we will be in heaven with him, but not yet. Now we live "upon the earth" (v. 5). What must we do? We must "put off" everything that is not Christlike, not after his image (v. 10). In us, as well as in heaven, Christ must be "all" (v. 11).

Question: As you read of all these unChristlike deeds, which one will you take action against?

Friday: Colossians 3:12–17

Here is a guide to Christian character. How do you rate? (a) *What you are* (vv. 12–15). This comes first, because it is the most important. The godly person is gentle, restrained, thoughtful. Are you? (b) *What you say* (v. 16). If your words are to be worth listening to, your mind must be stored with "the word of Christ." Then, whether speaking or singing, you will be a help to others. (c) *What you do* (v. 17). This verse gives a simple test which we can apply to everything we do. If we live this way, we shall not go far wrong.

Question: In what ways did Christ himself demonstrate this character?

Saturday: Colossians 3:18–4:1

Three great principles are to govern our relationship with each other. (a) *Obedience.* Notice this idea in 3:18, 20, 22. We are so independent these days that we don't like to obey. (b) *Justice.* "Fairness" is another word for it. See 3:21 and 4:1. We should do what is right, not what happens to be convenient. (c) *Love.* Although mentioned only in 3:19, this is to govern all our dealings with each other. And everything must be done "in the Lord" (3:18) and "to the Lord" (3:23).

Questions: Which group or groups do you come into? How can you apply these verses in you life?

Weeks 4 and 5—From God's Manual of Devotion

For the next two weeks we will concentrate on the personal devotional life as we read from the most precious devotional passages in the Bible, the book of

Psalms. Watch for two things: (a) *The place of the Word in the devotional life.* This comes mainly in the first week. Neglect of the Bible can starve one's Christian life and render it ineffective; (b) *The place of prayer in the devotional life.* This is our emphasis in the second week. We will see the many forms of prayer and the blessings that spring from it.

Week 4

Sunday: Psalm 119:9–16

You and Your Bible. This psalm is rich in teaching on how to use God's Word. (a) *Read it!* Make it your delight (v. 16); rejoice in it (v. 14); seek the Lord's face in it (v. 10). (b) *Hide it!* Store it up deep within you (v. 11); memorize it; meditate on it and turn it over in your mind (v. 15). (c) *Obey it!* Test your life by it (v. 9); use it to help you forsake sin (v. 11); guide your steps by it (v. 10). (d) *Declare it!* Pass it on to others and let its truth govern all you say (v. 13).

Question: How many things can you find in these verses that God's Word will do for us?

Monday: Psalm 119:97–104

The writer of this psalm tells us how God's Word affects: (a) *His head* (vv. 98–100). What three groups of people are mentioned? The thoughtful reader of God's Word is wiser than all. No teacher can substitute for the Word. (b) *His feet* (vv. 101–102). The Scriptures direct his steps into God's ways. (c) *His mouth* (v. 103). Time with the Bible sweetens his nature and his language. (d) *His heart* (vv. 97, 104). Through meeting the Lord in the Word, this godly man comes to *love* the Bible and *hate* all that goes against it.

Question: What do you learn from each of the *names* given to the Bible in these verses?

Tuesday: Psalm 1

Taking in and giving out. No one can give out something completely different from what he or she takes in, and this psalm gives us two alternatives. (a) *Feeding on the world.* Note the danger in verse 1 of soaking up the spirit of godless society and taking on its appearance. See in verses 4–6 the end of that way. (b) *Feeding on the Word.* By contrast, the man in verse 3 is like a tree that drinks constantly from the water of the river. The meaning is in verse 2. Constant meditation in God's Word leads to a fruitful life.

Questions: How much time do you spend with your Bible daily? Do you "meditate day and night"?

Wednesday: Psalm 19

(a) *God known in the skies* (vv. 1–6). The brightness of the sky and the sun mirror the glory of the Lord who made them. How blind the man who cannot see it! (b) *God known in the Scriptures* (vv. 7–11). Knowledge of God from nature can never bring salvation; for that, we need the Word. It converts the soul (v. 7) and points the way to blessing (v. 11). (c) *God known in the soul* (vv. 12–14). As the Word goes deep into our soul, so does the cleansing and keeping power of the Lord (vv. 12–13). We become a fit place for him to dwell.

Questions: Have you ever prayed the prayer of verse 14? How far has it been answered up to now?

Thursday: Psalm 42

One reason for reading the Bible is that it deals with all our varied needs. Today's psalm, for instance, deals with *depressions*. (a) *The experience.* "My soul is cast down within me" (v. 6). Find verses that speak of hopeless longing, sadness, craving for past days, nameless anxieties, utter helplessness, bewilderment. It is an all-too-common experience today. (b) *The answer.* Grasp the truth that God is not dead (v. 8)! The tunnel will have an end. Light will come. Meanwhile, hold on tight to the God who saved you (vv. 5, 11).

Question: Is it a sin to be depressed?

Friday: Psalm 63

"Early will I seek you." Make this your daily watchword! But do not come casually or merely out of duty; come earnestly, with real longing (v. 1). Notice three phrases: (a) *"My soul thirsts"* (v. 1). If you have no thirst to know your Lord better, question whether you know him at all. (b) *"My soul shall be satisfied"* (v. 5). Read the promise of Proverbs 8:17. May this be your daily experience. (c) *"My soul follows hard"* (v. 8). Yes, you need persistence, both to seek God in the Word and to serve him in the world.

Question: How much are we told about the Lord in this psalm?

Saturday: Psalm 65

As you read the verses from day to day, ask yourself, "What do they tell me about God?" Today we have: (a) *His graciousness* (vv. 1–4). List the blessings God has for the one who belongs to him. (b) *His greatness* (vv. 5–8).

His power is seen as creating, sustaining, and governing everything in all the world. (c) *His goodness* (vv. 9–13). He prepares the ground for sowing, cares for growing plants, blesses the harvest, multiplies the flocks. All nature shouts and sings (v. 13).

Question: Are there spiritual blessings similar to the ones in verses 9–13?

Week 5

Sunday: Psalm 3

"I cried . . . he heard!" (v. 4). Those simple words sum up this psalm. (a) *"I cried!"* David's prayer consisted, first, of telling God frankly about his situation (vv. 1–2), and then reminding God of his own nature and promises (v. 3)—a good pattern for prayer. (b) *"He heard!"* David says this first by *faith;* and because he believes God will answer, he sleeps peacefully (v. 5). This is in spite of the fact that he is still surrounded by enemies (v. 6). This is what is sometimes known as *the rest of faith,* and prayer is an essential part of it.

Question: What should we do when people say of us what they said in verse 2?

Monday: Psalm 23

(a) *What a Guide* (vv. 1–3)! Prayer for guidance will always be answered if prayed with a sincere intention to obey. These verses can come true for every one of us. (b) *What a Guard* (v. 4)! The child of God walks through this life surrounded by divine protection. The devil's darts cannot touch us, even in the trial of death itself. (c) *What a God* (vv. 5–6)! He is overflowing with blessing for his children, more than "my cup" can ever hold (v. 5), both in this life and the next (v. 6).

Question: How many blessings are there in this psalm that we can confidently pray for?

Tuesday: Psalm 28

Prayer Clears the Air. As David begins to pray, the storm clouds seem to be all around him. (a) *Looking downward* (vv. 1–5). See how preoccupied he is with problems, with people who do not care about God, and with his fears for the future. Now prayer turns his thoughts to the Lord. (b) *Looking upward* (vv. 6–9). Immediately the clouds begin to lift. The Lord's presence becomes real (v. 6), fellowship with the Lord becomes a delight (v. 7), and David rejoices in being one of God's people (vv. 8–9). Yes, "prayer changes things"!

Question: How different do things look to *you* after you have prayed?

Wednesday: Psalm 32

Confession in Prayer. Unconfessed sin seriously hinders the Christian walk and witness. Notice the order here. (a) *Sin*. See the effect sin had on David's life (vv. 3–4). He found no peace of soul. (b) *Confession*. His spirit broken, David got down before the Lord and opened his heart. He told all, kept nothing back (v. 5). (c) *Forgiveness*. In Christ, we may *know*—not think or hope, but *know*—that we are forgiven! (d) *Guidance*. When no sin is interrupting the lines of communication with God, he can guide our footsteps once again (vv. 8–9).

Question: Do we have to *work* for forgiveness, or is it a *gift?* See Romans 4:5–8.

Thursday: Psalm 34: 1–10

Praise leads to proclamation. Like David we should get into the habit of talking about the wonderful things God has done for us, and talking in two ways. (a) *Telling God about them in thanksgiving.* Nothing stimulates prayer like praising! Remember often to begin prayer times by recalling outstanding recent blessings (vv. 4, 6). (b) *Telling others about them in testimony.* Letting our praises flow does wonders in loosening our tongues to speak of him to sinners (v. 8), to saints (v. 9), and in fact to all (v. 10).

Question: Which verse will you choose from today's portion to memorize?

Friday: Psalm 34:11–22

A condition of blessing. There are many promises of blessing in these verses, but did you notice to whom the promises are made? Over and over again we are told they are for "the righteous." To be righteous depends on two things: (a) *Faith.* To turn from one's sins (v. 18) and place one's trust in the Savior (v. 22) is the first essential doorway to God's favor; (b) *Obedience.* Righteousness does not just exist "on paper"; it means practical obedience to the Lord's will (vv. 11–14) in everyday matters.

Question: Underline the promises made here to the righteous. Which one speaks most clearly to your own heart?

Saturday: Psalm 150

Underline the word praise in this psalm. How many times does it occur? How should God be praised? (a) *By everyone.* If you have "breath," you should use it to praise the Lord (v. 6). (b) *For everything.* For blessings material and spiritual, blessings of heart and home; for every way in which "his power . . . his mighty acts . . . his excellent greatness" have come to you. (c) *In every way.* Let us not become stereotyped in the ways we praise the Lord. David didn't (vv. 3–5).

Question: If you were compiling a psalm of praise like this one, how would *you* express *how* and *why* God should be praised?

Week 6—Paul, a Model Witness

"Not the gospel of God only, but also our own souls" (1 Thessalonians 2:8). The main thrust of our readings in 1 Thessalonians this week will be the character of a true witness for Jesus Christ. We are not so much concerned with the "how" as with the "who," because, in the last analysis, witnessing is not a technique. It is men and women telling their friends and fellow sinners the best news ever told. And for *that* kind of work, it matters much what kind of person you are.

Sunday: 1 Thessalonians 1:1–10

Witnessing in power. When Paul and Silas had come to Thessalonica, their witness for Christ had certainly been effective. It had resulted in *conviction* (v. 5), in *conversion* (v. 9), and in *continuance* (vv. 3, 10). Notice that their witness was *prayerful* (v. 2) and *powerful* (v. 5). What power was it? Not human power, but Holy Spirit power (v. 5). But how was it seen? Not in great oratory or fiery speech, but in *"what manner of men we were"* (v. 5). It was the power of God seen in their transformed lives.

Questions: How does your life look to those you witness to? How much has it been transformed by power from on high?

Monday: 1 Thessalonians 2:1–12

Witnessing in love. These are remarkable verses. They show us that Paul's witness in Thessalonica was completely conceived and nourished in *love*. There was *no* concern for himself (v. 2), *no* unspiritual means of persuasion (v. 3), *no* wooing of the Thessalonians with flattery (vv. 4–5), *no* desire for any personal advantage (v. 5), *no* longing for any personal success (v. 6), *no* hope for any material return (v. 9). He cared for nothing but to introduce them to Christ and to let the friendship ripen. How this puts to shame our love of numbers, prestige, and converts we can show off.

Question: What is your motive in witnessing for Christ?

Tuesday: 1 Thessalonians 2:13–20

Witnessing in fortitude. There are two great themes here: (a) *Persecution*. Notice again what opposition Paul had to face (vv. 14–16). Many Christians today are too spineless to face opposition and triumph over it. They give up the first time they encounter difficulty or resistance. But not Paul; (b) *Perseverance*. Paul just went on speaking the Word of God, and what happened (v. 13)? He was quite ready to throw himself back into the battle (vv. 17–18). And his joy was all the greater in the end (vv. 19–20).

Question: Can you give an example of a time when you have gone on witnessing faithfully in a difficult situation?

Wednesday: 1 Thessalonians 3:1–13

Witnessing in persistence. Paul was no fly-by-night witness. He did not lead the Thessalonians to Christ and then leave them to make their own way. He gave them: (a) *His love.* He went on loving them (vv. 5, 8). Notice what he says of himself in verse 12; (b) *His friend.* If he himself was prevented from going to them, he sent someone else who could help them (v. 2); (c) *His advice.* He taught them in the way of Christ (vv. 12–13); (d) *His prayers.* He prayed for them earnestly and constantly (v. 10). His interest never slackened.

Questions: What to you do next with someone you have led to Christ? For how long do you follow up?

Thursday: 1 Thessalonians 4: 1–12

Witnessing in holiness. When we lead someone to Christ, what kind of Christian will he or she turn out to be? Today's passage makes clear that the person will most likely follow the example he or she has "received of us" (v. 1). A sobering thought! (a) *Lust must be rejected.* God's word emphasizes that absolute purity, in thought and speech and deed, must be seen in a Christian's life (vv. 3, 7). (b) *Love must be reflected.* Paul's love for the Thessalonians is mirrored in their love for each other and for others (vv. 9–10).

Question: Notice the expression "more and more" in verses 1 and 10. What does it tell you about the Christian life?

Friday: 1 Thessalonians 4:13–5:11

Witnessing in hope. Paul's witness made much of the

fact that Christ would return for judgment on the unbelievers, and to bring eternal blessedness to his own. We
saw that this teaching played a big part in the
Thessalonians' conversion (1:9–10). Now we see: (a) *the
comfort of Christ's coming.* Twice Paul mentions the
word (4:18; 5:11). Underline in the passage the truths
that bring comfort; (b) *The challenge of Christ's coming.*
In 4:13, 5:4, 6, 8 find at least four practical implications
of the coming of Christ.

Question: Do you find Christ's future return an inspiration to you in your witness?

Saturday: 1 Thessalonians 5:12–28

Witnessing in fullness. Witness must not end with a
"three-point gospel." It must include the *fullness* of
God's wonderful revelation in Christ, such as: (a) *church
life* (vv. 12–15), for God sets his children in the family
of the church of Jesus Christ; (b) *devotional life* (vv. 16–
20), for this is the foundation of daily Christian living;
(c) *sanctified life* (vv. 21–24), which, as you see, includes
our part and God's; and (d) *outgoing life* (vv. 25–28), as
we build each other up in the grace of Christ.

Question: How much of the Christian life is a personal matter and how much a corporate matter?

Week 7—How to Live for Christ

This week we read two chapters from Romans in
which the Lord gives us basic principles to follow in
spiritual Christian living. Watch for two sides to this:
(a) *Inward experience.* We read how God's Spirit can fill
our hearts and fit us for a Christlike life; (b) *Outward ex-*

pression. The inner life of the Spirit is openly demonstrated in the detail of daily obedience.

Sunday: Romans 8:1–8

(a) *Death to the old way!* Paul calls on us to be done with old, non-Christian ways of living. At best they depend on trying harder, making efforts, obeying rules. Paul calls this living by the law. It leads to failure, condemnation, and death. (b) *Long life the new way!* There is "no condemnation" this way (v. 1). Sin was dealt with on Calvary (v. 3), and the Spirit of our Lord Jesus frees us from all bondage (v. 2). The fresh wind of the Spirit blows within us. We are alive (v. 6)!

Questions: Do you know anything about this kind of living? Are you still trying to succeed the hard way—the old way?

Monday: Romans 8:9–17

(a) *Life in the Spirit.* The Spirit of God dwells in the heart of every one who belongs to Christ (v. 9). See what he gives: *life,* flowing forth in righteous living (v. 10); *assurance,* for the Spirit's presence is obvious and is our guarantee that God accepts us (v. 16); *victory,* for he is the Spirit of power and can conquer the deeds of the body (v. 13). (b) *Led by the Spirit.* This is the other side of the coin (v. 14). If we do not follow his direction, we will not be free to do his work.

Question: Read verse 17. What does it mean to you when Paul says we are "heirs of God and joint-heirs with Christ"?

Tuesday: Romans 8:18–27

(a) *Groaning now!* Life in the Spirit does not mean a

bed of roses. The whole creation in which we live is in bondage (v. 20) and is groaning in pain (v. 22), so we ourselves are bound to feel it to some extent (v. 23). But verses 26–27 show us one way to find release. (b) *Glory hereafter!* Verse 18 sums up the contrast, and verse 21 tells us that glory is waiting, not only for us who belong to Christ, but also for the whole of the natural creation. So the key words are *hope* (v. 24) and *patience* (v. 25). The greatest blessings are still to come.

Question: What do we learn about prayer from verses 26–27?

Wednesday: Romans 8:28–39

Victory. Victory is the underlying thought of all these verses. For example: (a) *Victory over our circumstances* (vv. 28–30). There is no chance or misfortune in the Christian's life. We see the hand of God in all; (b) *Victory over our critics* (vv. 31–34). God stands foursquare for his people, and every slander against them will be put to silence; (c) *Victory over our calamities* (vv. 35–39). Are we prepared to face distress, famine, even death itself, for Christ? He will lead us safely through.

Question: What have you learned about being an overcoming Christian?

Thursday: Romans 12:1–8

The dedicated Christian life. Test yourself in three ways. (a) *The nature of dedication (vv. 1–2).* It is separation *from* the spirit of the world and consecration *to* the will of God. Have you done it? (b) *The spirit of dedication* (vv. 3–5). It is possible even to be proud of one's dedication. Let verse 3 speak personally to your heart. (c) *The results of dedication* (vv. 6–8). What is dedicated to the service of God must be used in the service of others. Which gifts in these verses are you exercising?

Questions: What is meant by "a living sacrifice" (v. 1)? Have you learned to view your life this way?

Friday: Romans 12:9–15

Three themes are woven together here. List them or underline them in different ways in your Bible. (a) *My new life and myself.* Which phrases tell me ways in which the new life will show itself in my own heart and life? (b) *My new life and my Lord.* I have a new longing to satisfy him with my service. (c) *My new life and my brother.* How are other people going to be affected by the fact that I am now animated by a new, Spirit-empowered life?

Question: Humility, sympathy, kindness, joyfulness— which two words best sum up the message of today's verses?

Saturday: Romans 12:16–21

(a) *Don't try to push yourself higher!* It is so silly to try to exalt oneself. It means very little when you look at it from the Lord's point of view (v. 16). It brings no joy to you or to others. The way of verse 18 is much better, and only comes through lowliness of mind. (b) *Don't try to push others lower!* If it has to be done at all, it is the Lord's job, not yours (v. 19). Getting even is not a Christian concept (v. 21). How must we treat those who make themselves our enemies (v. 20)?

Question: If I learn to treat others this way, what effect is this likely to have on myself?

Weeks 8 and 9—The Triumphant Christian

"The Lord your God fights for you" (Joshua 23:10). For two weeks we will be reading about Joshua's campaign to conquer Canaan. The story is full of sound principles that will help us in our own "warfare." As you read these chapters, remember: (a) *our enemy* is Satan and his forces (compare Ephesians 6:12); (b) *our Captain* is the Lord Jesus (compare 2 Timothy 2:3–4); (c) *our weapons* are spiritual, such as prayer, faith, obedience, the Word of God (compare 2 Corinthians 10:4). These weapons will lead us to victory in Jesus Christ.

Week 8

Sunday: Joshua 1:1–9

(a) The call. Here we have the thrilling fact that it is God who calls us to a life of victory. It is his will for us, for every one of us. Read verse 5 again and make it your own. (b) The challenge. A spirit of defeatism will not help us on the road to victory. Notice God's repeated command to Joshua (verses 6, 7, 9). (c) The condition. Joshua's whole campaign had to be grounded in God's Word (v. 8). Note the three steps in his use of the Bible; he was to read, meditate, and obey. Follow these steps daily.

Questions: How many promises of God can you find in these verses? How does each one apply today?

Monday: Joshua 1:10–18

(a) *The need for cooperation.* It does not often happen

that a Christian is expected to win victory *alone*. Usually there is a fellowship, within which he or she learns to fight against Satan and to win battles for the Lord. This means that friction and strife within the fellowship will greatly hinder our warfare. Today we read Joshua's call for support and harmony. (b) *The need for courage*. First, *the Lord* had said it (v. 7). Now Joshua's *friends* say it (v. 18). So let us strengthen each other along the way.

Question: Why is it wrong for a Christian to be self-centered?

Tuesday: Joshua 2:1–6, 23–24

Know your enemy! Do not neglect to find out all you can about Satan and his devices. (a) *Know his strength*. Never make the mistake of underestimating the devil. Get to know where he lurks, what his weapons are, and how he fights. Learn from others who have been defeated—and from your own defeats! (b) *Know his weakness*. Know that he is a defeated foe, and that he trembles before your Captain (v. 24). Learn the best tactics for overcoming him, and use them every chance you get.

Questions: Who is the one and only true conqueror of Satan (v. 24)? How can we share his victory?

Wednesday: Joshua 5:13–6:5

An interview with the Lord. The one who appeared to Joshua was the Lord Jesus himself, and without this personal interview the battle could never have been won. (a) *Sweet communion* (5:13–15). Joshua, away from the camp and the busyness of his daily life, spends time with the Lord, renewing his strength. (b) *Strict com-*

mands (6:1–5). This follows straight on; it is the Captain who speaks (v. 2). We must learn to recognize his voice and to follow his instructions to the letter.

Questions: Why did the man have his sword drawn in his hand (5:13)? What does this tell us about Christ?

Thursday: Joshua 6:12–20

(a) *The claim.* By circling the city day after day, Joshua's army claimed the city for the Lord. We do this by believing prayer. (b) *The confidence.* The "shout" and the "trumpets" typify the courage and expectancy with which we undertake any battle for the Lord. (c) *The conquest.* "They *took* the city" (v. 20). They did not win it by fighting. They just took what the Lord had given (v. 16). (d) *The consecration.* No God-given victory should be exploited for our own advantage or boasted about for our own glory (v. 19).

Question: In the Christian life, is there a time to wait (v. 14) and a time to act (v. 20)?

Friday: Joshua 7:1–6

Here is a chain of events that Israel too often experienced, and which has exact parallels in the Christian life. (a) *Departing from the Lord.* How easily, even in a moment of victory, we allow our hearts to be drawn away from our Master and to the cheap delights of this world. (b) *Defeat by the enemy.* Satan is on his toes and never lets an opportunity like this slip by. (c) *Despair in the heart.* There is no joy in compromise, only disappointment and ultimately utter despair. The application? Allow sin no foothold in your life.

Question: What was missing from the plan to attack Ai? Compare 9:14.

Saturday: Joshua 7:7–15

How could Israel get right with God? How could they ever have victory again? There was only one way. (a) *This was not a time for prayer.* Strangely enough, there are certain times when prayer has no value, and this is one of them. It is no use praying about defeats when there is willful sin not dealt with. (b) *This was a time for rooting out sin.* It must be pulled out like a decayed tooth, and no stump must be left to cause trouble again. Many Christians are defeated because they are half-hearted about this.

Questions: Is there a point at which you are regularly defeated? Just how ruthless are you about sin?

Week 9

Sunday: Joshua 7:16–26

(a) *A lesson for the non-Christian.* You have the story of sin briefly told in verse 21: "I saw . . . I coveted . . . took . . . hid." The ending of the story is in verse 25. If there is one message that is consistently taught throughout all Scripture, it is that "the soul that sins shall die" (Ezekiel 18:20). (b) *A lesson for the Christian.* When we think of the horror from which the Lord has delivered us, should we ever make any place in our lives for the sin that nailed our Savior to the cross?

Questions: What have you learned from the story of Achan? What is the main lesson for you?

Monday: Joshua 8:1–9

(a) *God makes a promise!* How different from the last time the Israelites attacked Ai. Then there had been a fatal weakness which had led to defeat. This time they had a sure promise of God which would lead them to victory (v. 1; compare 6:2) at the very point where they had been defeated before. (b) *Joshua makes a plan.* No hasty rush into a dangerous situation this time! Inspired and instructed by the Lord, Joshua thought out just what he would do and then acted on it in faith (v. 7) and obedience (v. 8).

Question: What are the main factors that make the difference between victory and defeat for the Christian?

Tuesday: Joshua 8:18–26

Why did the Israelites win this battle? *Was it because they took a larger army?* Compare verses 3 and 5 with 7:3. Verse 25 shows that the soldiers of Ai were much fewer in number. But that was not the reason. *Was it because they had a better plan?* Compare verses 19–20 with 7:4. They tricked the enemy into leaving the city undefended. But that was not the secret. *Was it because the Lord took control?* See verses 18 and 26. Yes, this made the difference. Not more will power, not better planning, but more complete dependence on the Lord is the secret of victory.

Question: Why did the men of Ai make such a bad mistake?

Wednesday: Joshua 23:1–10

May the Lord give each one of us as fine a testimony at the end of our lives as Joshua had. What three elements are found here? (a) *What the Lord had done.* So often a testimony concentrates on what "I" have done; but not Joshua's. (b) *What the Lord was still going to do.*

What great promises still remained to be claimed! The Lord has not changed. What he had done he would do again. (c) *What the people's response should be.* Check your own life against each of the words of counsel Joshua gave his followers.

Question: How do verses 9–10 apply in the life of a Christian today?

Thursday: Joshua 23:11–16

Joshua's last testimony continues. (a) *The faithfulness of God.* "You know in all your hearts and in all your souls, that not one thing has failed" (v. 14). Read the whole verse again. Can you say the same? (b) *The fickleness of men.* How sad that, having seen all the good things the Lord had done, the people were on the verge of forsaking the Lord! Note the warnings Joshua had to give them, and especially the consequences that would follow. That is why the first three words of verse 11 are so important.

Question: It is so easy to backslide, almost without knowing it. Do you test yourself regularly?

Friday: Joshua 24:14–21

(a) *A decision to be made.* Many people never realize that the decision for Christ involves putting him before every other master and every other love (vv. 14–15). The point of verses 16–18 is that he is worthy of this exclusive allegiance. What has he done for *you* that makes him worthy? (b) *A demand to be met.* What is demanded of anyone who decides to put the Lord first (vv. 19–21)? Consecration to the Lord means consecration to holiness—no compromise, no toying with sin, no second-rate standards.

Questions: Have you made a clear-cut decision like this? Can you say what Joshua said at the end of verse 15?

Saturday: Joshua 24:22–31

So a great man passed to his reward. His works lived on after him (v. 31). Verse 23 gives us a great saying of his, which was among his last words. (a) *It had a negative side*. "Put away, said he, the strange gods." Anything in our lives that means enough to us to affect our total obedience to the Lord is a strange god and must be put away. (b) *It had a positive side*. "Incline your heart unto the Lord." It is indeed a matter of the *heart*. If you allow your heart to pull you in another direction, disaster may result.

Question: Can you think of ways in which you could take steps to "incline your heart unto the Lord"?

Weeks 10 and 11—The Gospel Gets to Work

"You shall receive power . . . and you shall be witnesses" (Acts 1:8). Our readings in Joshua were concentrated on the way of victory in personal spiritual life. Now, as we turn to the early chapters of Acts, we see the triumphant experiences that await us as we proclaim the gospel to the outsider. In Acts, this happens especially through the outward-looking, Spirit-filled fellowship of the church. It can still happen today. Pray that it will, and that we may have a vital part in it.

Week 10

Sunday: Acts 1:1–12

Notice three personalities in this portion: (a) *Christian believers*. Two things about them: they have seen the risen Lord (v. 3) and they are commissioned to tell others about him (v. 8) until all have heard; (b) *The Holy Spirit*. His work is clearly set forth in the first part of verse 8, and we see his immense power at work as we read these chapters of Acts; (c) *The Lord Jesus*. He is alive today (v. 3), although we do not see him (v. 9). He is the subject of our witness (v. 8), and he will return to reign (v. 11).

Questions: According to today's portion, how do we know that Jesus is alive? Is it possible that we may be wrong?

Monday: Acts 2:1–13

Here we have the key to understanding the rest of the book of Acts. (a) *The disciples were empowered*. "They were all filled with the Holy Spirit" (v. 4). The promised power had come! This power is the birthright of every Christian, not the possession of a few. It led to open, joyful witness (v. 11). (b) *The people were amazed*. The disciples were so transformed that the people around could not think how it had come about! They started asking questions—and that opened the door for some answers!

Question: How much is there about your life that the unbeliever cannot possibly explain apart from Christ?

Tuesday: Acts 2:14–24

Seizing an opportunity. Peter takes his cue from the question, "What does this mean?" (v. 12), and preaches the gospel. (a) *He speaks from the Scriptures* (vv. 16–21). He is really saying: Why are you so surprised? It is all in the Bible! God's promises and the gospel invitation are plain for all to read (vv. 17, 21). (b) *He speaks about Christ* (vv. 22–24). In very few words, Peter gives a complete picture of the person and work of Christ. Quite right, Peter! *Christ* is the gospel, and all true preaching is about him.

Questions: How often have you opened your Bible with some non-Christian? When did you last talk to someone about Christ?

Wednesday: Acts 2:32–40

Today we have two important works of the Holy Spirit. (a) *He exalts Christ* (vv. 32–36). It is significant that immediately after being filled with the Spirit, Peter makes a declaration that gives Christ the supreme place (v. 36). This is a sure evidence of the presence of the Spirit. (b) *He convicts men* (vv. 37–40). *Where* were these men convicted (see v. 37)? *What* had convicted them (v. 36)? But most of all we must ask *who* had convicted them? It was of course the Holy Spirit. When the Spirit fills the Christians, outsiders are drawn to Christ.

Questions: What did Peter call upon his hearers to do? What would the result be?

Thursday: Acts 2:41–47

Look at these new converts! (a) *Beginning* (v. 41). Notice that they received the word, made an open confession, and joined the fellowship. (b) *Growing* (v. 42). Care was taken that they should continue in the faith and grow in grace. Note the means that were used. (c) *Expressing* (vv. 43–46). Toward others, this took the form of sharing; toward God, it was expressed in worship; and toward themselves, in gladness of heart. (d) *Multiplying* (v. 47). There were always new converts being added to the congregation!

Questions: Is your own church like this? What is your best contribution toward making it more so?

Friday: Acts 3:1–10

(a) *Open eyes*. How easily we "look right through" people without even noticing them or their needs! But Peter was watching for people who might cross his path, whom he might help to Christ. (b) *Open heart*. Nobody cared about a beggar; nobody paused to talk to him or help him, beyond tossing him a coin. Peter opened his heart to this man and shared Christ with him. (c) *Open lips*. What effect did his healing make on this man (vv. 8–9)? Public testimony and praise followed at once, as they always should.

Question: I know you are busy—so were Peter and John—but how much time do you have for individuals?

Saturday: Acts 4:1–13

Here are two qualities not only of Peter and John but also of the whole New Testament church. (a) *The boldness of their stand for Christ*. People noticed it (v. 13). We are given two reasons why Peter was so bold (beginning of v. 8 and end of v. 13). May both experiences be ours. (b) *The clarity of their word about Christ*. Peter is asked a question in verse 7, and instead of giving a rambling, indefinite answer, he speaks briefly and clearly about his Lord (vv. 9–12). Let us learn to put our beliefs in simple words.

Questions: Are you sure that you are "filled with the Holy Spirit"? How much time do you spend "being with Jesus"?

Week 11

Sunday: Acts 4:23–31

The fellowship of the believers in those early days must have been very real, and there is no reason why we should not enjoy the same fellowship today. (a) *It was a fellowship of prayer.* To turn from conversation to prayer was completely natural for them (vv. 23–24). Their prayer was based on God's Word (vv. 25–26), and was for themselves and each other (v. 29). (b) *It was a fellowship of witness.* This was never far from their thoughts (v. 29). It was not their own troubles that filled their minds, but the pressing need to speak the gospel to a needy world.

Question: How often do you pray with your Christian friends?

Monday: Acts 4:32–37

(a) *Self was submerged.* That is the main truth in this story of early Christian "sharing." Personal possessions no longer meant anything—the Lord was all in all. So, of course, there was a cheerful spirit of giving to meet each other's needs. They laid down no rules about it; their hearts just overflowed with love for each other.

(b) *Grace was given.* The more we *use* God's grace, the more it is given (v. 33). The more we give, the more we get. The more we share, the more God shares with us.

Questions: How much do personal possessions mean to you? Could you cheerfully give them away if necessary?

Tuesday: Acts 5:1–11

But these early Christians were still human! (a) *Why was their sin so serious?* Was it just the sin of imitating someone else more spiritual than themselves (compare vv. 1–2 with 4:36–37)? Was it just a desire to be thought well of? Verses 3, 4, 9 reveal the point of the sin; it was fraud against *God. All* hypocrisy is. Beware of it. (b) *Why was their punishment so severe?* We are not told that they lost their salvation, but their terrible punishment makes clear for all time what God thinks of this kind of sin.

Question: Do you long to *appear* more spiritual than you really are?

Wednesday: Acts 6:1–8

(a) *Note the work of Satan.* Things were going badly for him (5:42). So he attacked. His plan was to set everyone thinking and talking about church organization (v. 1) so that the preaching of the Word would be neglected (v. 2). He does the same today. (b) *Note the work of Stephen.* The answer was to appoint a working committee of Spirit-filled men (v. 3) to look after the whole matter so the preaching might continue (v. 4). Chief among these men was Stephen, who did this lowly task so faithfully that the Lord soon gave him greater work to do (v. 8).

Question: What kind of men were chosen (v. 3)?

Thursday: Acts 8:1–12

(a) *Great persecution* (v. 1). Acts 7:59 tells what happened to Stephen, and it led to "great lamentation" (v. 2). But those early disciples never *feared* persecution. And they never let it stop them from preaching Christ (vv. 4–5). (b) *Great joy* (v. 8). Philip took over where Stephen left off. How simple his preaching was! What did it consist of (vv. 5, 12)? But how supreme his power was; much greater than Simon's (v. 10), for it was the power of Christ, able to transform lives (v. 7).

Questions: Do you react to opposition by speaking about Christ more and more? Does God do "miracles" through you?

Friday: Acts 8:13–25

(a) *The true.* Many people were truly converted in Samaria. They trusted in the name of the Lord Jesus; they were baptized into him; and they received the Holy Spirit (given in this special case by means of the apostles). (b) *The false.* Simon *seemed* to be truly converted. He believed and was baptized (v. 13). But he did not trust in Christ with all his heart, so his baptism meant nothing. His life was not changed (v. 18), and his state was desperate (v. 23). There were true and false in the church even then.

Questions: What do you think Simon was really interested in? What should he have been concerned about?

Saturday: Acts 8:26–40

(a) *A man looking for God.* Even today, all around us, there are people longing to find God. But often they do not know *the right place to look*. The Ethiopian had found it—the Bible (v 28)! This is the mine in which the treasure of the gospel is found. People do not know *the right thing to do*. But the Ethiopian found this too—he believed in Jesus with all his heart (v. 37). (b) *A man looking for men*. Philip sets us a fine example. He was alert, ready to speak to this seeker; he preached Jesus (v. 35, compare v. 5); and he led the man to a decision (v. 37).

Question: Have you ever led someone to Christ like this?

Week 12—The Way Ahead

Perhaps more than any other epistle in the New Testament, 1 Peter was written *"that you may grow"* (1 Peter 2:2). It urges us to continue with Christ, and it helps us to do so. We will read selections from it this week to see something more of the way that lies ahead of us. As we read each day's portion, let us pray that we may faithfully follow the way it shows us.

Sunday: 1 Peter 1:1–9

The way of endurance. We are shown that the way is not going to be easy. But first we are encouraged. (a) *A mighty calling*. Verses 1–5 are packed full of the many blessings we have through our calling to belong to Christ. How many can you see? Which have already taken place? Which are happening now? And which are still to come? (b) *A mighty conflict*. Verses 6–9 turn to the hard life we are often called to lead in this world. We are often in "heaviness" (v. 6), but what is the answer to it (v. 8)?

Question: What evidences do you find in these verses that the Christian life is to be a joyful one?

Monday: 1 Peter 1:13–21

The way of holiness. Here are two reasons why we must be holy. (a) *Holy—because of what God is like.* Be very clear on this: "He that has called you is holy." We are children of an all-holy Father, and we are required to be absolutely like him (v. 15). It is not easy; we will have to be diligent (v. 13) and obedient (v. 140. (b) *Holy—because of what Christ has done.* Look what our former "vain conversation" (or evil life) did to Christ (vv. 18–19). His precious blood was shed for sin. Shall we continue to live in sin?

Question: What do we learn from today's verses about the person and work of Christ?

Tuesday: 1 Peter 1:22–2:5

The way of growth. Spiritually, we are newly born (1:23) and need to grow up (2:2). (a) *Keep coming to the Word.* Note what the Word has already done for you (1:23). It has given you new birth by bringing you the gospel (1:25). Now read 2:2. The Word has now become your food, and if you are to grow you cannot do without it. (b) *Keep coming to the Lord.* Perhaps what you know of him so far is just a "taste" (v. 3)! Now, as you keep coming (v. 4), you will be built up in your Christian faith.

Question: Examine carefully the command of 2:1. Have you already laid these things aside, or are traces of them left?

Wednesday: 1 Peter 2:18–25

The way of patience. Let's face it: if we are Christians there are going to be times when we will be misunderstood and maltreated. (a) *An experience we must learn* (vv. 18–20). What kind of suffering does *not* bring credit on the Christian or his Lord (first half of v. 20)? But what kind *does* please God (second half of the verse)? Yet this is the hardest kind to bear. (b) *An example we must follow* (vv. 21–25). Which half of v. 20 do *Christ's* sufferings come under? What was his attitude (v. 23)? And the result (v. 24)?

Questions: Have you ever run into this experience? How did you make out? Are you prepared for the next time?

Thursday: 1 Peter 3:8–16

The way of courtesy. Here is sound advice. (a) *What you don't say* (see vv. 9–10). "Evil" is anything springing from the devil rather than from God. "Railing" is insulting language. "Guile" is deceitful cunning. There is nothing like this when the Christian lives close to the Lord. (b) *What you do say.* A "spiritual" tongue speaks graciously, and always brings blessing into the lives of others (vv. 8–9). Note in verse 15 what else the tongue is ready to do.

Question: Many Christians are unwise in the use of their tongues, speaking tactlessly, foolishly, or hurtfully. Are you careful about this?

Friday: 1 Peter 4:7–13

The way of watchfulness. As we grow in Christ, we

think more of the fact that he will soon return, and we live in the light of that coming. (a) *We look to the Lord* (v. 7). We are more and more concerned to keep in prayer fellowship with him. (b) *We look to each other* (vv. 8–11). Our love deepens for those with whom we will spend eternity, and we do all we can to build them up in Christ. (c) *We look to the future* (vv. 12–13). Things of earth become less and less important, viewed in the context of eternal joy and glory.

Question: Does the Lord's coming regularly affect your thinking and living, or do you forget it for long periods?

Saturday: 1 Peter 5:1–11

The way of victory. We have a fine note on which to end. (a) *A word to the "elder."* Look after the younger ones; don't despise them, but help them, not boastfully but humbly (vv. 1–4). (b) *A word to the "younger."* Don't be too sure of yourself; learn from older Christians. Above all, learn from the Lord your God (vv. 5–7). (c) *A word to all.* Avoid the one who will harm you; watch for Satan's devices, and stand against them. But seek the One who will establish you; use every means to learn of the Lord and to draw upon him (vv. 8–11).

Questions: Are you growing in Jesus Christ? How are you planning for your further growth?

CONTINUING STEPS IN THE CHRISTIAN FAITH

Now that you have experienced the joy and enrichment that comes through a daily quiet time, you will want to continue. We suggest that you subscribe to the *Daily Bread*. This excellent devotional guide is issued quarterly by Scripture Union. You may write to them at 1885 Clements Road, Unit 226, Pickering, Ontario L1W 3V4.